T0319698

Pensions and Population Ageing

Pensions and Population Ageing

An Economic Analysis

John Creedy

Truby Williams Professor of Economics, University of Melbourne, Australia

Edward Elgar
Cheltenham, UK • Northampton, MA, USA

Published by
Edward Elgar Publishing Limited
8 Lansdown Place
Cheltenham
Glos GL50 2HU
UK

Edward Elgar Publishing, Inc.
6 Market Street
Northampton
Massachusetts 01060
USA

A catalogue record for this book
is available from the British Library

Library of Congress Cataloguing-in-Publication Data
Creedy, John, 1949–
    Pensions and population ageing : an economic analysis / John
Creedy.
    Includes bibliographical references.
    1. Aged—Government policy—Econometric models. 2. Old age
pensions. 3. Demographic transition—Economic aspects.
4. Expenditures, Public—Econometric models. 5. Social security-
-Econometric models. I. Title.
HD7105.3.C74   1998
331.25'2—dc21

                           97-39374
                              CIP

ISBN 1 85898 802 0

Printed and bound in Great Britain by Biddles Ltd, Guildford and King's Lynn

Contents

List of Figures

List of Tables

Acknowledgements

This book relies heavily on a number of papers, many of which have been written with joint authors. My major debt is to those collaborators. Section 1.2 of Chapter 1 uses material from Creedy and Disney (1989a). Other related joint work with Richard Disney on pensions includes Creedy and Disney (1989a, b, c; 1990; 1992) and Creedy, Disney and Whitehouse (1992); this has not been used directly in this book but has been important in its genesis. Chapter 2 uses material from my introduction to Creedy (1995). Chapter 3 is based on Creedy and Taylor (1993). Chapter 4 is based on Alvarado and Creedy (1995); a full-length treatment of these and related issues is in Alvarado and Creedy (1997). Chapter 5 is based on Creedy and Morgan (1993, 1995). Chapter 6 is based on Creedy and van de Ven (1997). Chapters 8 and 9 are based respectively on Creedy (1994a, b). Chapter 10 draws on Atkinson, Creedy and Knox (1995a), and is also influenced by Atkinson, Creedy and Knox (1995b, 1996). Chapters 11 and 12 are based respectively on Atkinson and Creedy (1996, 1997). I am very grateful to these collaborators and to the various journals for permission to use the material here.

The research reported here has been supported by a number of grants. In particular, I am grateful to the Australian Research Council (for support under the 'small' and 'large' grants scheme), the Association of Super-annuation Funds of Australia (for the work on early retirement) and the University of Melbourne Faculty of Economics and Commerce.

I should also like to acknowledge the extensive editorial and word processing help provided by Kath Creedy in producing the camera-ready copy of this book.

Part I

Introduction

Chapter 1

Introduction and Outline

Increasing attention, stimulated by the awareness of population ageing, is being given to problems of pension finance and the analysis of alternative arrangements for the provision of retirement incomes. The purpose of this book is to examine several aspects of population ageing and pensions, with an emphasis on the design and use of simple economic models. Such models can often be used to focus on particular aspects of a very broad problem. The book is not meant to be comprehensive, nor does it attempt to provide an overall evaluation of the large literature or the many policy proposals which have been made: for such a comprehensive and integrated analysis, see Disney (1996).

Population ageing represents an important stage which many industrialised counties are likely to experience in the early years of the next century, having previously passed through several previous stages or demographic transitions. The nature of demographic transitions and their implications for the development of social insurance arrangements are discussed briefly in section 1.1. Section 1.2 examines the dependency ratio, which is widely regarded as a major indicator of population ageing. The discussion concentrates on the relationship between demographic and economic dependency. Section 1.3 completes this introduction by providing an outline of future chapters.

1.1   Demographic Transitions

It is possible to distinguish several demographic stages or transitions through which most industrialised societies passed. The time taken to move through the various stages has varied between countries, and there is evidence to suggest that more recently industrialised countries have passed through some later stages relatively more quickly. The different stages are characterised mainly by their birth and death rates (expressed per 1,000 of the population) and the associated age distribution of the population. They are shown in Table 1.1 under four main headings. The figures given in the table must be regarded simply as representative values rather than indicating precise orders of magnitude for a particular country.

The pre-modern stage is characterised in Table 1.1 by quite high fertility and high mortality. The expectation of life at birth is only about 25 years, so there are very few individuals in the 'over 60' age group. The high birth rate, while imposing heavy burdens on families, is nevertheless associated with a growth rate of the total population of only about half of one per cent, so that reproduction is sometimes described as being inefficient.

The middle two stages are shown as 'early transition' and 'later transition' periods, though they are sometimes amalgamated into a single demographic transition, or movement towards the 'modern' period. The early transition period is characterised by a fall in mortality, particularly infant mortality, which is associated with a rise in the expectation of life to about 30 years. In the later transition period, improved health conditions reduce mortality and increase longevity further, while the birth rate continues to be high. This period is thus associated with a high 'youth dependency' ratio, with about 45 per cent of the population under the age of 15 years. Despite the much higher expectation of life at birth, the proportion of people over 60 years remains relatively low, while the population growth rate is increased to about 3 per cent. Indeed, it can be shown that the extent of population ageing is more sensitive to fertility than to mortality changes.

The later transitional period, despite the increased longevity, is one in which the idea of retirement from employment does not really exist. Indi-

Table 1.1: Demographic Transitions

	Pre-modern	Early	Later	Modern
Births/1000	45	45	45	20
Deaths/1000	40	33	15	10
% 15 years and under	36	38	45	26
% 60+ years	5	5	5	15
Expectation of life at birth	25	30	50	70
Population growth rate	0.5	1	3	1

viduals continue to work, unless illness prevents labour market participation. For example, during this transitional period in Britain, the various friendly societies were able to cope with the requirements of such sickness insurance for their members, and were well placed to handle the potential moral hazard problems. Hence increased longevity did not lead to a breakdown of family support systems, despite the high 'youth' burden already faced.

As shown in Table 1.1, the modern period experiences a continued reduction in mortality and an increase in the expectation of life at birth to about 70 years. A significant feature is the reduction in the birth rate so that, despite the extra longevity, the population growth rate falls to about 1 per cent. The age composition of the population shifts dramatically, with a reduction in the proportion below 15 years and an increase in the proportion aged over 60 years. These later transitions place great strain on family support systems, given the difficulty of making life cycle savings, despite the reduction in the youth burden. In Britain, the significance of these changes was not at first fully appreciated by the friendly societies, which were initially opposed to the introduction of government old age pensions, but the demand for some kind of government pension became irresistible in the major industrialised countries at the turn of the century. The shift from family support to government support in the form of the tax and transfer system involves a complex range of factors, including the high costs, particularly health costs, of supporting the aged compared to those of the young. Hence the overall burden of dependency increased despite the reduction in birth rates.

The modern period shown in Table 1.1 corresponds to the industrialised countries around 1960, and must be augmented by a yet more modern or post-modern period through which many countries are currently passing. The expectation of life at birth has increased further and it has been found that the support costs (particularly health costs) rise dramatically for individuals over 75 years, who form a growing proportion of the population. The birth rates have also fallen further, implying significant population ageing in the early years of the twenty first century. This population ageing is also associated with the ageing of the members of the post-war baby boom. The implications of the more recent demographic transition are, however, more complicated than is often thought in popular debates.

The recent post-modern period has also seen a substantial increase in the labour force participation rate of women (partly associated with the lower birth rate) along with a certain amount of variability in unemployment rates. Following a shift of the 'aged burden' to the tax and transfer system during the modern period, the commonly expressed fear is that future working populations will renege on the 'implicit social contract' between generations. Intergenerational equity issues are therefore now receiving some attention. It is also of interest that, despite the much lower birth rate, more recent times have seen increased pressure from some quarters for a further shift of the 'youth burden' to the tax and transfer system. Others have expressed concern over such a shift, partly associated with what some commentators have referred to as a breakdown of the nuclear family. Many of the industrialised countries may be regarded as entering a territory the characteristics of which are very difficult to predict. The demographic transition is nevertheless likely to involve a continued transition in social insurance arrangements, which have experienced very little stability in their short history.

1.2   The Dependency Ratio

In the debate on population ageing much attention has been given to the dependency ratio, where it is conventional to define aged dependants as the group including all those over pension age (usually 65 for men and 60 for women). The denominator in calculating the aged dependency ratio is usually the number of those between 20 and retirement age. It is often assumed that movements in such a ratio, defined only according to the age distribution of the population, accurately reflect movements in 'true' dependency ratios. However, such an assumption is too simplistic as allowance must be made for factors such as labour force participation. Many official projections assume constant participation rates, yet reduced fertility is likely to be associated with a movements towards higher female participation rates. This section considers the relationship between demographic dependency and economic dependency, the latter taking account of changes in the labour force participation rate of workers and other dynamic factors.

1.2.1 A Dynamic Formulation

It is useful to work in terms of generations of workers and retirees. The relationship between the number of current dependents, P, and that of current workers, E, is determined by two parameters. The first, μ, is a survival parameter governed by the expected average duration of retirement of each retiring cohort. The second, θ, is the proportion of the labour force, L, that participates in paid work. Thus:

$$P = \mu L_{-1} \tag{1.1}$$

and

$$E = \theta L \tag{1.2}$$

The size of the current and previous generations of the labour force, L and L_{-1}, are linked by the rate of population growth n since:

$$L = (1+n) L_{-1} \tag{1.3}$$

Substituting (1.2) into (1.3) and then using (1.2) lagged one generation gives:

$$E = (1+\varepsilon)(1+n) E_{-1} \tag{1.4}$$

where $(1+\varepsilon)$ denotes (θ/θ_{-1}) so ε is the growth of the labour force participation rate. Similarly, substituting for L_{-1} from the lagged form of (1.2) into (1.1) gives:

$$P = (\mu/\theta_{-1}) E_{-1} \tag{1.5}$$

Dividing (1.5) by (1.4) gives:

$$\frac{P}{E} = \frac{\mu/\theta_{-1}}{(1+\varepsilon)(1+n)} \tag{1.6}$$

which is a more appropriate measure of dependency than P/L.

However, equation (1.1) assumes that all members of the potential labour force, L, receive a pension, whether or not they participate in paid work. An alternative and simpler formulation is to write:

$$P = \mu E_{-1} \tag{1.7}$$

This case typifies a 'pure' social insurance system in which pensions are only received by those who participate. The model in this case is considerably simplified as all terms in θ drop out, including ε, and $(1+n)$ combines the effects of population growth and any changes in the participation rate. Although in theory this case may be thought to correspond more closely to insurance schemes in developed countries, in practice pure insurance schemes are hard to find, given the presence of additional non-insurance benefits such as dependant's allowances and means-tested benefits. For this reason (1.5) is preferred here.

The components of the replacement ratio, b and w, are also related. Suppose that the benefit, b, is set as a proportion, β, of the wage earned by the retirees in their work life, z. Then:

$$b = \beta z_{-1} \tag{1.8}$$

The average wages of the current and previous generations are also linked by the rate of growth of real wages, g, so that:

$$z = (1+g) z_{-1} \tag{1.9}$$

Dividing (1.8) by (1.9) gives the replacement ratio in terms of β and the growth of real earnings:

$$\frac{b}{z} = \frac{\beta}{(1+g)} \tag{1.10}$$

The overall tax rate, τ, needed to finance pensions is equal to the replacement rate multiplied by the dependency ratio. Using (1.10) and (1.6) respectively gives an expression for τ as:

$$\tau = \frac{\beta\,(\mu/\theta_{-1})}{(1+n)\,(1+g)\,(1+\varepsilon)} \qquad (1.11)$$

This formula has an intuitive rationale. The average tax rate needed to finance pensions is determined by the fraction of earnings replaced, β, and by the ratio of survivors to previous workers (μ/θ_{-1}). The higher the last ratio, the higher the current tax rate needed to finance the pension of survivors.

The value of τ is reduced if any of the three growth rates in the denominator are positive. The equation can again be simplified where pensions are only paid to retired workers, when θ_{-1} and $(1+\varepsilon)$ drop out. Furthermore, not only is there an upper bound on E which ultimately constrains ε, but in a steady state $(1+\varepsilon)$ must be exactly offset when pensions are only paid to retired workers, as these extra workers will ultimately receive the pensions which are accrued. However, many of the issues of pension policy that arise are better suited to the above dynamic framework, in which the growth rate of participation may be non-zero, than to comparative statics of steady states.

Finally, for generality, it can be noted that (1.11) can be simplified if it is assumed that benefits are indexed to earnings, which is less common, and not to prices as in (1.10). In this case $(1+g)$ drops out of the denominator and one more degree of policy flexibility is lost. The derivation of more complex indexation arrangements is discussed by Rosen (1984).

A policy issue stemming from this model concerns the interdependence of the growth rates g, n and ε, which is one of the most interesting and complex issues in this framework. For example, the growth of the labour force and productivity may be interdependent, although the form of the relationship is not clear *a priori*. Furthermore, the growth of labour force participation may be affected by the growth of real wages: this relationship might be expected to be positive in the short run if real wage rises induce greater participation, especially among married women. On the other hand, a higher rate of population growth may be associated with lower labour force participation especially among women of child-bearing age.

The growth rate of the tax rate as the population ages is alleviated significantly if a falling population growth rate leads to an increase in real wages.
This stimulates participation both indirectly by lower non-participation due
to child-rearing and directly by raising real wages if labour supply curves
are forward-sloping. This might be regarded as a 'virtuous circle' associated
with population ageing, but other outcomes are of course possible.

1.2.2   Some Numerical Examples

To illustrate the magnitudes involved, this subsection presents some numerical examples. A problem is that the growth rates in the denominator of
(1.11) are defined over generations without any specification of the duration
of a generation in years. Suppose, therefore, that the working life is 40 years
and the expected average duration of retirement is 15 years. The survival
parameter μ is therfore 0.375. If it is assumed that all men and half the
women were employed in their working life, θ is 0.75. Finally assume that β
is 0.5. If there is no growth in the population, in labour force productivity
or in labour force participation, the required tax rate, τ, is 25 per cent.

Consider next the dynamic aspect of the pension financing problem. Assume initially that the population grows at 1 per cent per annum through
labour force entry, productivity grows at 2 per cent per annum, and that
paticipation rates are constant. If discrete generations are considered, the
tax rate needed to finance the retirement of a given generation declines ex-
ponentially in line with population and productivity growth. The length of
this retired duration can be considered to be the expected duration of retirement, which, in this example, is 15 years. Thus the average tax rate needed
to finance the pensions of these retired generations is:

$$\frac{0.5\,(0.375/0.75)}{(1.01)\,(1.02)\,(1.00)^{15}} = 0.16 \tag{1.12}$$

This gives a rate of 16 per cent, considerably lower than in the static case.
It can be noted that this result is equivalent to that obtained from an overlapping generation model in steady state growth where the size of the cohort

does not enter (1.11) directly. The tax rate varies out of steady state as changes in the population growth rate work their way through the age distribution of the working life and retirement.

A change in the survival parameter, μ, affects both the numarator and the denominator. Thus a rise in the expected duration of retirement, say from 15 to 20 years, raises the tax rate needed to finance the scheme through the change in the numerator, but lowers it through the denominator, since the growth rates are now compounded over a longer period. In fact the former effect dominates (with $\beta = 0.5$, the required tax rate rises from 16 per cent to 18.4 per cent). But the relationship between the tax rate and increasing longevity is non-linear because the increased longevity occurs at the end of the life. In contrast, changes in β have linear effects on the tax rate.

It is also useful to consider the case where the growth rates are interdependent. Suppose that the population growth rate falls by the one percentage point from the previous example, to zero growth. Also assume that the elasticty of productivity growth with respect to population growth is -1, of participation with respect to population growth is -2, and of participation with respect to productivity growth is +1 (this is the virtuous circle case described earlier). This reduction in population growth reduces the tax rate needed to finance pensions by stimulating productivity growth and labour force participation growth. The consequent average tax rate in this case is 10.2 per cent.

In contrast, suppose the elasticity of productivity growth with respect to population growth is +1, with the other elasticities as before. Here the various effects of changes in population growth counteract each other, but the net effect is to raise the necessary tax rate slightly from the baseline case slightly to 18.6 per cent. Thus the tax rate is sensitive to the assumptions made concerning the relation between population growth and productivity growth.

1.3   Outline of Future Chapters

The remainder of this book is divided into three parts. Part II concentrates
on modelling ageing and social expenditure. Projections of the ratio of social
expenditure to Gross Domestic Product indicate the extent of the 'burden'
of aged care on future workers and have been used by governments to aid
policy decisions in such areas as immigration and superannuation. The basic
analytics of population growth and age structure are explored in chapter 2,
along with the link with social expenditure. Projections for Australia are
examined in chapter 3, where it is shown that the ratio of social expenditure to GDP is heavily dependent on assumptions made about real spending
growth, productivity growth, unemployment and participation rates. The
framework developed in chapter 3 makes the assumptions underlying the
projections clear and enables the results of changing the assumptions to be
easily compared.

The benchmark projections of the ratio of social expenditure to GDP assume constant age distributions of unemployment and participation rates,
constant real spending and productivity growth. According to these assumptions, the social expenditure to GDP ratios in Australia rise markedly
only after 2011. Chapter 3 uses sensitivity analysis to show that altering
the benchmark assumptions regarding real expenditure growth, productivity
growth and unemployment and participation rates causes significant changes
in the social expenditure to GDP ratio.

It should be stressed that projections of this kind provide only a partial
view of the types of problem that may be faced by policy makers. They
illustrate only the orders of magnitude of expenditure requirements which
result from demographic and other changes. A more complete analysis would
require the detailed treatment of revenue considerations. Population ageing
will have implications for the tax base, so that tax *rates* do not necessarily
have to follow the expenditure ratios.

The demographic projections used in chapter 3 depend significantly on
assumed migration flows, as well as fertility and survival rates. In view of the
importance of migration in the Australian context, this aspect forms the focus

of chapter 4. On the basis of census data which show that the fertility and mortality characteristics of overseas migrants do not adjust immediately but take several generations, chapter 4 extends traditional analyses of migration by using a decomposition of the population. This decomposition makes it possible to study the impact on population structure of changing not only the level but also the composition of the migration intake.

The analysis shows that, although the composition of the net intake does play a role in determining the ethnic structure of the population, the level of overseas migration exerts the most significant impact on the size and age structure of the population. Increasing the intake of migrants reduces significantly the proportion of elderly people throughout the projection period.

Part III concentrates on the analysis of pensions and pension finance, and examines several types of economic model. It begins in chapter 5 by examining the relationship between tax rates and pension levels in alternative pay-as-you-go state pension systems. Debates concerning population ageing have typically focused on a very simple model in which there is an obvious relationship between pension levels, the aged dependency ratio and the income tax rate. The chapter shows that the range of policy choices available to governments is substantially greater, given the number of relevant policy variables. Furthermore, the nature of the government's budget constraint is rather complex, so that the trade-offs are not immediately obvious. Hence illustrative orders of magnitude are reported. After presenting a general analysis of the government's budget constraint it concentrates on two basic types of scheme. The first, using a means-tested pension and only income taxation, is similar to the Australian scheme; the second is closer to the flat-rate component of the UK pension scheme, and has consumption and payroll taxes in addition to income taxation, but no means-testing.

For representative parameter values, it is found that an increase in the pension of $1,000 in the means-tested scheme requires an increase in the income tax rate of just under one-half of one percentage point. When there is no means-testing, the required increase in the income tax rate is just over one-half of one percentage point. In the means-tested system, an increase in the threshold income level, above which the benefits are reduced, of $1,000, requires an increase in the income tax rate of just under one-fifth of one percentage point. In the multi-tax (no means-testing) scheme, an increase in the consumption tax rate of one percentage point is associated with a decrease in the income tax rate of about nine-tenths of a percentage point. The difference partly reflects the fact that the tax base for consumption is slightly lower than for income taxation. However, an increase in the payroll tax rate of one percentage point is associated with a decrease in the income tax rate of about one and one-fifth of a percentage point. Despite the upper limit on the payroll tax, this is applied to gross income, unlike the income tax which has a tax-free threshold.

Chapter 6 turns to the question of the conditions under which social transfers can increase welfare, compared with private savings, in the context of overlapping generations models. The standard model generates a simple condition involving the real interest rate and the growth rates of incomes and population. Chapter 6 extends the standard model by allowing for increased longevity and labour supply variations.

Chapter 7 considers some of the basic market failure arguments used to justify a state pension system. It examines the incentives to contract out of a government scheme which involves some intra-generational redistribution between individuals. It is shown how a stable scheme requires some contributions by those who are allowed to contract out.

Chapter 8 compares alternative state pension schemes using a two-period framework which allows for labour supply responses to changes in the tax and transfer structure. It is found that a two-tier pension scheme gives rise to a non-convex budget constraint facing individuals, giving rise to an interesting range of labour supply responses. An increase in the proportional pension rate used in the second tier (the earnings-related component) is found to increase aggregate labour supply, despite the rise in the tax rate needed to finance the extra pensions. The existence of an earnings-related component in a pension scheme therefore has a positive incentive effect and raises average earnings in comparison with a flat-rate pension.

Chapter 8 also examines the maximisation of a social welfare function specified in terms of individuals' utility levels, and considers the trade-off between average utility and its inequality. It is found that the trade-off displays a 'backward-bending' section whereby, above a certain tax rate, further increases in the tax rate both reduce average utility and increase inequality. A major result is that, in terms of the trade-off between equity and efficiency implied by the social welfare function adopted, the flat-rate pension dominates the two-tier pension. A higher social indifference curve can always be reached using a flat-rate pension. Although analytical results cannot be obtained, this result is found to be robust in the face of variations in parameter values.

Chapter 9 examines compensating wage differentials for an individual worker in a two-period framework in which labour supply is endogenous. Comparisons are made for a flat-rate pension and a two-tier scheme, and allowance is made for the existence of taxes and other transfer payments. The results generate quite different elasticities according to assumptions made regarding tastes of the individual, and particularly the wage rate. In addition, the elasticities of earnings with respect to pensions can take both positive and negative values. The empirical literature on compensating variations has ignored labour supply effects and has concentrated on double-log regressions of earnings on pension costs and other characteristics of workers and firms, and has been looking for a coefficient on the logarithm of pension costs of minus unity. The failure to obtain this result was first explained in terms of the data and estimation method used, and was then later attributed to the bias arising from unobserved individual characteristics.

Chapter 9 argues instead that the basic specification used in empirical studies is inappropriate, along with the *a priori* expectation that the existence of compensating wage differentials implies a (negative) unit elasticity. Using a utility-maximising lifetime model, it is shown that the appropriate elasticities are sensitive to assumptions regarding preferences, particularly the level of wage rates. A model of individuals' behaviour is examined explicitly, paying attention to the tax structure as well as the pension structure, along with the endogeneity of labour supply. The results suggest a degree of pessimism regarding the ability to measure empirically the extent of such variations using standard regression techniques.

Part IV turns to the analysis of alternative pension arrangements using a lifetime simulation model. Simulations are required in view of the lifetime framework and the complexity of tax and transfer systems. Chapter 10 discusses the issue of lifetime income equality under alternative retirement income arrangements, with particular reference to Australia. The advantage of using Australia is that the government funded age pension is fully means-tested and thereby provides a contrast with schemes where part or all of a basic pension is paid to all aged persons. With many governments considering an increase in the level of means-testing, the Australian experience provides valuable insights.

The results show that the introduction of a universal pension coupled with significant changes and simplifications to the structure of taxation and superannuation have little effect on the redistributive impact of the tax structure in a life-cycle framework. The analysis of lifetime inequality does not find substantial differences in the redistribution of lifetime income associated with means-testing and other features of the taxation system. It is therefore not possible to conclude that the use of a universal, rather than means-tested, age pension significantly affects inequality. Alternative structures for the provision of retirement incomes are considered which embody hybrids of the current Australian system and other systems in place worldwide. Results show that it seems possible to eliminate complexities from the current system without having any deleterious effect on equity. It is also found that the progressivity of a system is more sensitive to the characteristics of individual behaviour following retirement, and the post-retirement mortality experience, than the presence or otherwise of means-tests for the age pension.

Chapter 11 presents simulation results of allowing individuals to optimise their retirement behaviour, in terms of the allocation of assets, under various conditions. It is found that the current structure of taxation and retirement income provision in Australia does not provide a clear incentive to purchase annuities. Further, it is shown that alternative schemes incorporating a universal pension polarise optimal behaviour away from choices which provide low levels of retirement income, and which are driven by the means test.

It is also shown that the current scheme has no clear advantage over these alternatives in terms of equality or progressivity. Other schemes providing a universal pension are more successful in providing incentives to purchase annuities and imply a lower penalty for those whose mortality experience is higher, typically those with lower lifetime earnings.

Chapter 12 examines the optimal choice both of the retirement age (between the ages of 55 and 65) and the allocation of assets at retirement. Each simulated member of a cohort is assumed to maximise a lifetime utility function defined in terms of the present value of utility, with each year's utility defined in terms of consumption and leisure.

In view of the fact that individuals' preferences are not known and the simulation model requires a number of strong simplifications and assumptions, the results must be treated with caution. However, they suggest the existence of a significant incentive towards early retirement and a substantial impact of the age pension means-tests on the allocation of resources and optimal retirement age of individuals. The extent and nature of incentives are found to vary with the mortality assumption used, and depend on the means-tests associated with the age pension. The assumptions of a universal pension encourages later retirement in a substantial proportion of the cohort. The analysis raises the question of the appropriate level of contribution rates in a mandated scheme. Results suggest, not surprisingly, that lower contribution rates encourage a later preferred retirement age.

The analysis of pensions presents many complex problems. An aim of this book is to demonstrate how reasonably simple economic models can be designed and used to shed some light on the issues.

Part II

Ageing and Social Expenditure

Chapter 2

Population Ageing and Expenditure

The purpose of this chapter is to present some of the simple analytics of population growth and structure, involving the relationships among the age structure and fertility, mortality and migration patterns. A basic framework of analysis is presented in section 2.1. The age structure of the population has implications for social expenditure growth, given that most of the components of social expenditure are age-related. However, there are many interdependencies involved in the link between age structure and social expenditure. A framework of social expenditure analysis is presented in section 2.2. The population projections made using the results of section 2.1 can be used as inputs into the framework of section 2.2 in order to produce projections of social expenditure per capita. Some numerical examples are provided in section 2.3.

2.1 Population Projections

2.1.1 A Social Accounting Framework

This section examines some of the basic determinants of the population age structure and population growth. Population flows can be represented by a social accounting framework, shown in Table 2.1. The square matrix of flows from columns to rows has $N - 1$ non-zero elements which are placed

Table 2.1: Demographic Flows

Age	1	2	3	...	N	Births	Entrants	Total
1	0	0	0	...	0	b_1	v_1	p_1
2	f_{21}	0	0	...	0	0	v_2	p_2
3	0	f_{32}	0	...	0	0	v_3	p_3
...	...	...	...	...	...	...	...	...
N	0	0	0	...	0	0	v_N	p_N
Exits	d_1	d_2	d_3	...	d_N			
Total	p_1	p_2	p_3	...	p_N			

on the diagonal immediately below the leading diagonal. No one is assumed to survive beyond the age of N. Define the coefficients, a_{ij}, showing the proportion of people in the jth age who survive in the country to the age i as:

$$a_{ij} = f_{ij}/p_j \tag{2.1}$$

only the $a_{i+1,i}$, for $i = 1, ..., N-1$, are non-zero. This framework applies to males and females separately, distinguished by subscripts m and f. The 'forward equations' corresponding to this framework are therefore:

$$p_{m,t+1} = A_m p_{m,t} + b_{m,t} + v_{m,t} \tag{2.2}$$

$$p_{f,t+1} = A_f p_{f,t} + b_{f,t} + v_{f,t} \tag{2.3}$$

Given population age distributions in a base year and information about the relevant flows, equations (2.2) and (2.3) can be used to make projections. In general the matrices A_m and A_f, along with the births and inward migration flows, may be allowed to vary over time. Changes in the As can arise from changes in either mortality or outward migration.

Further specification can be added to the model by considering births. Suppose that c_i represents the proportion of females of age i who give birth per year. Many elements, for young and old ages, of the vector, c, will of course be zero, and in general the c_is may vary over time. Suppose that a proportion, δ, of all births are male, and define the N-element vector τ as the column vector having unity as the first element and zeros elsewhere. Then births in any year can be represented by:

$$b_m = \delta \tau c' p_f \tag{2.4}$$

$$b_f = (1 - \delta)\tau c' p_f \tag{2.5}$$

where c' is the transpose of the vector c (that is, the column vector written as a row). The b vectors contain only one non-zero element, of course. Equations (2.2) to (2.5) can thus be used to make population projections for assumed immigration levels.

2.1.2 Stable Populations

If all the coefficients, represented by the elements of the A matrices and the c and v vectors, remain constant over time the population eventually reaches a stable level and age distribution. The age distribution of males and females will be such that total 'entrants' are exactly matched by total 'exits' from the country. In practice, such a stable population is unlikely ever to be experienced, given the time required for convergence from some initial non-stable distribution, so that the coefficients are bound to change before stability is reached. Yet it is sometimes useful to have an idea of the population structure towards which any given system may be thought to be approaching.

First, consider the female population. Combine (2.3) and (2.5) and set $p_{f,t+1} = p_{f,t} = p_f$. With constant migration, $v_{f,t} = v_f$ per year, so that:

$$p_f = [A_f + (1 - \delta)\tau c']p_f + v_f \tag{2.6}$$

Notice that the matrix $\tau c'$ takes the simple form:

$$\tau c' = \begin{bmatrix} c_1 & . & . & c_N \\ 0 & . & . & 0 \\ & . & & . \\ & . & & . \\ & . & & . \\ 0 & . & . & 0 \end{bmatrix} \tag{2.7}$$

Rearranging (2.6) gives:

$$[I - A_f - (1 - \delta)\tau c']p_f = v_f \tag{2.8}$$

where I is the unit matrix. It is convenient to denote the matrix in square brackets in (2.8) as M, so that:

$$Mp_f = v_f \tag{2.9}$$

This matrix takes the form:

$$M = \begin{bmatrix} 1 - (1 - \delta)c_1 & -(1 - \delta)c_2 & -(1 - \delta)c_3 & .... \\ -a_{21} & 1 & 0 & .... \\ 0 & -a_{32} & 1 & 0 \\ ..... & ..... & ..... & ..... \end{bmatrix} \tag{2.10}$$

The first few terms c_i (for $i = 1, ..., N$) are, as noted above, zeros. However, this matrix is in general non-singular, so that the stable female distribution is given by:

$$p_f = M^{-1}v_f \tag{2.11}$$

The model has the property that if there are no inward female migrants, so that $v_f = 0$, then equation (2.9) represents a set of linear homogeneous equations. Given the non-singularity of M, this means that the model has only the trivial solution whereby the stable population is $p_f = 0$.

If $v_f = 0$, and denoting the matrix in square brackets in (2.6) as A_f^*, then:

$$p_{f,t+1} = A_f^* p_{f,t} \tag{2.12}$$

and continual substitution gives:

$$= \left(A_f^*\right)^t p_{f,t+1} \tag{2.13}$$

Therefore with constant birth and death rates and no migration, the total population grows at a constant geometric rate (which may be positive or negative) while the relative age distribution settles down to be constant whatever the form of $p_{f,1}$. The population growth will either be 'explosive' or converge to zero, which again confirms the earlier result. The population grows steadily if the largest characteristic root of A_f^* is greater than unity, and declines steadily if the largest root is less than one. The process shown in equation (2.13) can converge to a stable value of p_f only if the matrix A_f^* has a largest characteristic root of exactly unity, which is extremely unlikely.

The stable male population is determined by substituting (2.4) into (2.2) and setting the coefficients constant, so that:

$$p_m = A_m p_m + \delta \tau c' p_f + v_m \tag{2.14}$$

Substituting for p_f from (2.11) and further rearranging gives:

$$p_m = [1 - A_m]^{-1} \left[\delta \tau c' M^{-1} v_f + v_m\right] \tag{2.15}$$

A stable non-trivial solution for p_m does not therefore require any male migrants.

2.2 Social Expenditure

It has been mentioned in chapter 1 that an increase in longevity in the industrialised countries led to a demand for the introduction of some kind of government age pension and health insurance scheme. The difficulty of providing adequate personal savings for old age, combined with the strain placed both on family support and the existing sickness support schemes (which anyway covered a small minority of workers), resulted in a situation in which the aged formed the vast majority of those found to be living below a designated poverty level. At around the same time, there was much wider recognition of a role for the government in the other areas of social insurance, such as sickness and unemployment. It is no accident that this movement coincided with wider support for redistribution, involving also the use of progressive income taxation.

Social insurance schemes are typically financed on a pay-as-you-go (PAYG) basis, that is from current taxation, and pensions form by far the largest component of social expenditure. A variety of market failure arguments have been advanced to justify the use of such social insurance. In addition, the inter-generational transfers involved in PAYG pension schemes are often described in terms of an implicit social contract between three generations: each generation stands to gain from such an arrangement so long as there is sufficient productivity and population growth. It is widely anticipated that the increased ageing of the population, which is expected to be most prominent in the early years of the next century, will place great strain on this metaphorical contract.

Pensions and health are not the only age-related forms of social expenditure, so the implications of population ageing for aggregate social expenditure are far from clear, given the many elements involved. Many projections can perhaps be criticised for not providing sufficient sensitivity analyses, given the wide range of assumptions and the many uncertainties involved. A projection framework which formalises the approach used by a number of investigators may be described as follows.

As before, the population is divided into N age groups and the numbers in each group at time t placed in a vector p_t, where $p_t = p_{m,t} + p_{f,t}$. The social expenditures per capita within each group are placed in a matrix with N rows and k columns, where there are k items of social expenditure (education, medical care, pensions and so on). If this matrix is denoted S, then the i, jth element s_{ij} measures the per capita cost of the jth type of social expenditure in the ith age group. Suppose that the jth type of social expenditure per capita is expected to grow in real terms at the annual rate ψ_j in each age group. Then define g_t as the k-element column vector whose jth element is equal to $(1 + \psi_j)^{t-1}$. Aggregate social expenditure at time t, C_t, is thus equal to:

$$C_t = g'_t S' p_t \qquad (2.16)$$

where, as above, the prime indicates transposition. This could be extended by allowing for expenditure per person in each category and age to differ for males and females, but such information is rarely available.

The relevant cost is not the absolute value as in (2.16), but the ratio of this cost to GDP in each year. Projections of Gross Domestic Product depend on assumptions about five factors: initial productivity, defined as GDP per employed person, productivity growth, employment rates, participation rates and the population of working age. Total employment is the product of the population, participation rates and the employment rate. Employment is calculated by multiplying the labour utilisation rate by the labour force. If U_t is the total unemployment rate in period t, the utilisation rate is $1 - U_t$. The aggregate unemployment rate is calculated by dividing the total number of unemployed persons in period t, V_t, by the total labour force in that period, L_t. The value of V_t is in turn calculated by multiplying the age distribution of unemployment rates by the age distribution of the labour force, where these differ according to both age and sex.

Let the vectors U_m and U_f be the N-element age distributions of male and female participation rates. If the symbol $\wedge$ represents diagonalisation, whereby the vector is written as the leading diagonal of a square matrix with other elements equal to zero, the total number of people unemployed in period t is:

$$V_t = U'_{m,t} \hat{L}_{m,t} p_{m,t} + U'_{f,t} \hat{L}_{f,t} p_{f,t} \qquad (2.17)$$

The labour force in period t, L_t, is given by:

$$L_t = L'_{m,t} p_{m,t} + L'_{m,t} p_{f,t} \qquad (2.18)$$

Suppose productivity grows at the constant rate, θ. Then GDP in period t is calculated as the product of the utilisation rate, $1 - U_t = 1 - V_t/L_t$, the labour force, L_t, and productivity, whence:

$$GDP_t = \left\{ \frac{GDP_1}{(1 - U_1)L_1} \right\} (1 + \theta)^{t-1} (1 - U_t) L_t \qquad (2.19)$$

If the population age distribution, along with the sex and age specific participation and unemployment rates, are constant, then the social expenditure
to GDP ratio remains constant if all items of expenditure grow at the same
rate as productivity; that is, if $\theta = \psi_j$ for $j = 1, ..., k$.

   This framework illustrates that many assumptions are required to make
projections, and many potential interdependencies which are not easy to
model. For example, productivity may itself depend on social expenditures
and the age distribution of workers. Furthermore, participation rates and
population growth are interdependent. The changing age distribution is just
one component of the ratio of aggregate social expenditure to GDP, and its
effects may be swamped, for example, by changes in unemployment rates.

2.3   Hypothetical Examples

The demographic and social expenditure frameworks outlined above can be
illustrated by considering a hypothetical example where for simplicity there
are just five age groups. Suppose the constant survival rates for males and
females and the fertility rates are as shown in Table 2.2. With no migration
and the additional assumption that half of all births are male, the application of the population projection method gives a constant rate of population
growth of 1 per cent, with age distributions as shown also in Table 2.2. Suppose there are just four categories of social expenditure, nominally defined as
education, labour market-related (including unemployment benefits), health
and pensions. Hypothetical costs per capita are shown in Table 2.3. Suppose
male participation rates are zero for ages 1 and 5 and 0.95 for the other ages,
and female participation rates are 0.7, 0.7 and 0.4 for the middle three age
groups. Furthermore, assume that unemployment rates are 0.05 for all age
groups for males and females. If labour productivity is initially 180 units,
and both productivity and all social expenditures per capita grow at a constant rate of 0.018, then total social expenditure as a rate of GDP is found

Table 2.2: Population Structure 1

Age	Survival		Fertility	Age distrib		Total
	M	F		M	F	
1	0.990	0.990	0	0.2484	0.2453	0.2468
2	0.955	0.955	0.950	0.2434	0.2403	0.2418
3	0.755	0.775	0.755	0.2300	0.2272	0.2286
4	0.625	0.655	0.550	0.1719	0.1742	0.1731
5	0	0	0	0.1063	0.1130	0.1097

Table 2.3: Social Expenditure per Capita

Age	Education	Labour	Health	Pensions
1	10	0	5	0
2	8	5	4	0
3	0	5	5	0
4	0	5	12	5
5	0	0	20	25

to be constant at 0.2185.

Consider the alternative survival and fertility rates shown in Table 2.4. These rates represent lower mortality and fertility and imply a steady rate of population growth which is negligible, and a stable relative age structure as shown in Table 2.4. It can be seen that the population in this alternative case is substantially older than in Table 2.2. With the same assumptions about productivity, unemployment and so on, as in the first case, this new population structure implies a ratio of social expenditure to GDP of 0.2394. Hence population ageing in these examples implies increased total expenditures as a proportion of GDP. These orders of magnitude reflect those of the major industrialised countries.

The higher expenditure requires correspondingly higher tax revenues and, depending on the tax structure, increases in tax rates. This may perhaps generate pressure for some items of social expenditure to be reduced, for example, by cutting state pensions and government health benefits.

It is, however, most unlikely that the changes in the population structure would occur without any other changes, for example in participation rates.

Table 2.4: Population Structure 2

Age	Survival		Fertility	Age		Total
	M	F		M	F	
1	0.990	0.990	0	0.2335	0.2215	0.2274
2	0.955	0.955	0.90	0.2312	0.2193	0.2251
3	0.800	0.900	0.75	0.2208	0.2094	0.2150
4	0.780	0.855	0.47	0.1767	0.1885	0.1828
5	0	0	0	0.1378	0.1612	0.1498

Furthermore, social expenditures are also influenced by productivity and other variables. If the participation rates of women, in the middle three age groups, is increased to 0.8, 0.8 and 0.5 respectively, the social expenditure ratio would become lower, at 0.2247. If, in addition, all unemployment rates were 0.04, the ratio would be lower, at 0.2223.

Higher productivity would of course reduce the ratio further, though a differential between expenditure growth of each category and productivity means that the ratio falls steadily over time. What is clear is that population ageing is just one component of the aggregate social expenditure to GDP ratio, which is sensitive to a wide range of variables. Some of the variables, such as unemployment rates, may be independent of ageing, but there are several interdependencies about which very little is known. Nevertheless, the approach described here can be used to examine the sensitivity of results to alternative assumptions, and thus to identify those elements which require further detailed attention. The method is used in the following chapter to examine social expenditure projections for Australia.

Chapter 3

Social Expenditure Projections

This chapter uses the approach outlined in the previous chapter in order to examine the effects of the ageing population on government social expenditures in Australia as a percentage of GDP. Such projections have been made by Heller *et al.* (1986) for a variety of countries, and by Kelley (1988) and EPAC (1988) for Australia. Kelley (1988, p.40) concluded that 'Australia faces a relatively favourable demographic future. The widely publicised concerns about the difficulties of financing social services with an ageing population are less severe here than in most OECD countries.' This chapter uses more recent data and a more detailed breakdown of expenditure categories. It produces projections that are higher than those obtained by Kelley. This chapter also provides a more extensive examination of the sensitivity of results to alternative assumptions.

Projections of the social expenditure to GDP ratio are an important indication of the necessary government revenue which must be raised by future taxes. It is also important to be able to observe the effects on the projections of altering the assumptions. The framework used for projecting social expenditure to GDP ratios makes the underlying assumptions clear and enables the effects of changing these assumptions to be compared. The essential details of this framework is developed in section 3.1, while more details are in chapter 2. The data used are described in section 3.3. Benchmark projections are presented in section 3.4. Section 3.5 reports the sensitivity analysis undertaken, where real spending growth, productivity growth and unemployment and participation rates are altered from their benchmark levels.

3.1   The Framework of Analysis

3.1.1   Projecting Social Expenditure

The three major influences on public expenditure are the size of the population (which depends on fertility, mortality and immigration), changes in social policy which cause outlays in various government spending programmes
to change, and real increases or decreases in outlays due to factors other
than policy changes. For example, total social spending increases, even if
per capita spending does not grow in real terms and if social policy is not
altered, if the number of recipients increases. If the population remains constant and there is no change in social policy, but real spending per capita
rises over time, total social expenditure rises. In order to show the effect
of changing one of these factors in isolation, the relevant data are organised
into a population vector, a matrix for social expenditure per head in the
base period and a vector of growth factors for the different types of social
expenditure.

The population data for period t are contained in a vector, p_t, where the
jth element is the total population in the jth age group, for $j = 1, N$. This
is divided into males and females so that in each time period, t, the total
population can be defined as the sum of two N-element vectors, one representing the male population age distribution, $p_{m,t}$, the other representing the
female population age distribution, $p_{f,t}$.

The number of age-related spending categories is k, each of which is divided into spending on each of the N age groups. The social expenditure
matrix, S, contains data for government spending per head in each expenditure area and age group. Therefore, S has N rows and k columns and
the element in the ith row and jth column is the amount of spending per
head in age group i in category j. The framework could be extended to
allow government outlays to be disaggregated by sex, but these data are not
available.

Government outlays per head may vary in real terms over time for several reasons. For example, per capita health costs may rise, and a rise in future unemployment rates would cause spending per head on both unemployment benefits and employment programmes to increase. The framework incorporates this type of effect by using a vector of growth factors. Let the growth rate per year to be applied to any spending category be represented by ψ_j in the jth expenditure category $(j = 1...k)$; the growth factor for category j is thus $1 + g_j$. From the base period, $t = 1$, until time period t, social expenditure grows $t - 1$ times. Hence, the growth factor for spending category j corresponding to period t is given by $(1 + \psi_j)^{t-1}$. These can be placed in a vector g_t. Total social expenditure in time period t is represented by the scalar C_t and is calculated using:

$$C_t = g_t'S'p_t \tag{3.1}$$

where the prime indicates transposition (writing rows as columns and vice versa).

3.1.2 Projecting GDP

Projections of Gross Domestic Product depend on assumptions about productivity in the base period, defined as GDP per employed person, and its growth, along with employment rates, participation rates and the population of working age. Total employment is the product of the population, participation rates and the employment rate. The framework does not allow for endogenous interdependencies, such as the possible influence of education spending on productivity growth, or of pension policy on participation rates. However, such interdependencies may be accommodated when specifying the various rates used in the projections.

Unemployment rates are available by both age and sex. Male unemployment is the product of male age-specific unemployment rates, male age-specific participation rates and the male population age distribution. Female unemployment can be similarly found using female age-specific unemployment rates, age-specific participation rates, and the female population age distribution. Let the vectors $U_{m,t}$ and $U_{f,t}$ be the N-element age distribution of unemployment rates for males and females respectively. Likewise, let $L_{m,t}$ and $L_{f,t}$ represent the N-element age distribution of male and female participation rates. If the symbol $^\wedge$ represents diagonalisation, whereby the vector is written as the leading diagonal of a square matrix with other elements equal to zero, the total number of people unemployed in period t, V_t, is therefore:

$$V_t = U'_{m,t}\hat{L}_{m,t}p_{m,t} + U'_{f,t}\hat{L}_{f,t}p_{f,t} \qquad (3.2)$$

The total labour force in time period t, L_t, is calculated by multiplying male and female population age distributions by age and sex-specific participation rates and summing their products. Thus:

$$L_t = L'_{m,t}p_{m,t} + L'_{f,t}p_{f,t} \qquad (3.3)$$

The aggregate unemployment rate U_t, is therefore endogenous, and is calculated by dividing the total number of unemployed persons, using (3.2), by the total labour force, using (3.3). The number of people employed in period t, M_t, is equal to the labour utilisation rate, $1 - U_t$, times the labour force, L_t.

Productivity in period t is found by multiplying productivity in the base period, defined as the ratio of GDP to employment, by a growth factor, D, which is expressed in terms of the assumed annual growth rate, θ, as follows:

$$D_t = (1 + \theta)^{t-1} \qquad (3.4)$$

Since productivity is the ratio of GDP to employment, GDP in time period t may be calculated as the product of $1 - U_t$, L_t, and productivity in year t. Hence the method uses the decomposition:

$$GDP_t \equiv (1 - U_t)(L_t)(GDP_1/M_1)D_t \qquad (3.5)$$

The projected social expenditure to GDP ratio for time period t is projected social expenditure in time period t, calculated using (3.1), divided by projected GDP for time period t, calculated using (3.5), giving the scalar, C_t/GDP_t.

3.1.3 Changes in Productivity Growth

The assumption regarding productivity growth is obviously important. The above results can be used to derive the percentage change in the social expenditure to GDP ratio resulting from a change in productivity growth alone. If productivity growth increases by x percentage points, the new social expenditure to GDP ratio will be:

$$\frac{C_t}{GDP_t} = \frac{g_t' S_{p,t}'}{\left(\frac{GDP_1}{M_1}\right)(1 + \theta + x)^{(t-1)}(1 - U_t)(L_t)} \tag{3.6}$$

The percentage reduction in the social expenditure to GDP ratio resulting from the change in productivity growth is therefore given by:

$$1 - \left\{\frac{1 + \theta}{1 + \theta + x}\right\}^{(t-1)} \tag{3.7}$$

3.1.4 Changing Labour Market Assumptions

Altering the age-specific unemployment or labour force participation rates will change total unemployment and total government spending on unemployment benefits. Unemployment or participation rate alterations will also affect GDP, and both of these effects should be considered when carrying out sensitivity analyses. The GDP effect is automatically taken into account in equation (3.5) through the effect on U_t or L_t. However, a change in the age-specific unemployment rates must be accounted for by altering the growth rate of real unemployment outlays per capita, that is the appropriate element of ψ.

The above framework allows for constant real growth per year in total unemployment expenditure per capita. However, there are several factors which can affect this growth rate. If benefits per unemployed person increase in real terms and the number of unemployed people remains fixed, total unemployment spending will grow positively. As well, any factor which causes the number of unemployed people receiving benefits in future to change will also affect the growth rate of public unemployment expenditure. If unemployment rates change without a change in the population or participation rates, the number of unemployed people will change. A change in the eligibility requirements for unemployment benefits will change the number of unemployment benefit recipients and thus change total spending on unemployment.

The question therefore arises of how variations in, say, unemployment benefits and unemployment rates can be examined in a consistent manner. If unemployment benefits paid to each unemployed person in period t are denoted b_t, and if s_t denotes the cost per capita of unemployment benefits in period t, then by definition:

$$b_t = \frac{s_t p_t}{p_t R_t U_t} \tag{3.8}$$

where U_t is the aggregate unemployment rate, p_t is the total population and R_t is the aggregate participation rate. Thus

$$s_t = b_t R_t U_t \tag{3.9}$$

If b, M and U change by the proportionate growth rates per year respectively of g_b, g_R and g_u, then the resulting growth rate of s, g_s, is given by:

$$g_s = (1 + g_b)(1 + g_R)(1 + g_u)^{-1} \tag{3.10}$$

Hence g_s can only be interpreted as the growth in unemployment benefits per unemployed person if g_R and g_u are both zero. Therefore, the various rates cannot be set independently.

The same kind of argument applies to the other components of social expenditure. The above discussion has been in terms of aggregate rates, but it would in principle be possible to disaggregate by age groups. However, the projection method imposes a growth rate on each component of social expenditure for all age groups. Given that the age distributions change over the period, the use of formulae such as (3.10) must be regarded as an approximation only. Nevertheless, it is better to use this approximation than to ignore the interdependence altogether. No such adjustment was made by Kelley (1988).

3.2 The Data

The projections are severely constrained by data availability. There are no data disaggregating public social expenditure by sex, and it was difficult to find a detailed breakdown of State government expenditure. The number of age groups used was determined by the best available data on government outlays; those were contained in a Commonwealth Department of Community Services and Health social expenditure survey (CDC 1990). Nine age groups were specified in this survey, most of which differ slightly from the age groups used in other published work, most notably the Australian Bureau of Statistics (ABS). The varying age divisions used in different data sources created difficulties in finding data with matching age groups. The time periods chosen correspond to census years. The base period, $t = 1$, is 1988. The other periods are 2001 $(t = 14)$, 2011 $(t = 24)$, 2021 $(t = 34)$ and 2031 $(t = 44)$.

3.2.1 Demographic Data

The ABS projections used for the male and female population vectors corresponding to each time period, $p_{m,1}$ and $p_{f,1}$ to $p_{m,44}$ and $p_{f,44}$, are presented in Tables 3.1 and 3.2. These data are from *Estimated Resident Population by Sex and Age, States and Territories of Australia, June 1988 and Preliminary June 1989* (ABS 1989c, Table 1, pp.3-6). The projections of the population are taken from *Projections of the Populations of Australia, States and Territories 1989 to 2031, series A and B* (ABS 1989b, p.40).

These series assume fertility of 1.83 children per woman for 1989, declining linearly to 1.78 in 1998 and remaining at this figure until 2031. Annual net migration is assumed constant at 125,000 per year, and the age distribution of migrants assumed for the ABS population projections is the average of net overseas arrivals for the three years 1986, 1987 and 1988.

Table 3.1: Benchmark Age Distribution: 1988-2011

| Age | 1988 | | 2001 | | 2011 | |
Group	M	F	M	F	M	F
0-14	1891.9	1798.7	2069.7	1965.4	2118.4	2010.1
15-24	1395.8	1340.3	1398	1330.2	1509.3	1434.2
25-39	2016.4	1989.7	2307.3	2261.4	2331.5	2270.5
40-49	1061.3	1007.1	1474.4	1455.5	1639.5	1608.3
50-59	770.1	739.6	1196.2	1157.5	1470.4	1459.1
60-64	359.9	369.4	410.5	407.2	635.6	640.2
65-69	292.7	330.3	330.6	346.5	469.6	481.4
70-74	212.6	267.9	297.3	330.9	340.2	369.7
75+	256.4	438.1	427.2	668.1	530.6	784.7

Given the lower average age of migrants, the Australian population is forecast to age less than many other industrialised countries. Nevertheless, over the whole period there is an increase of 55 per cent in the 50 to 59 age group, and an increase of 66 per cent in the number of males over the age of 75. Between 2001 and 2011, most growth seems to be in the 50 to 69 age bracket, with a 55 per cent rise in the 60-64 age group. In 2021 and 2031, there are significantly more males over the age of 65 than in the previous periods. The proportion of males in the 0-39 age groups falls between 1988 and 2031, and the proportion of the male population over the age of 70 rises from 1988 onwards. The percentage of the male population aged 60 and above rises after 2001.

For females, there is a significant rise in the 40 to 59 age group between 1988 and 2001, and the over-75 age group also increases markedly. From 2001 to 2011, the largest rise occurs in the 60 to 64 age group which increases by 57 per cent. Between 2011 and 2021, the number of females in the 70-74 age group shows a marked rise. The proportion of females in the 0-39 age group falls in each period, whereas the proportion of females in the 70 and above age group rises. Like the male population, the percentage of females over the age of 60 rises after 2001.

An indication of the effect of the ageing population on the labour force

Table 3.2: Benchmark Age Distribution: 2021-2031

	2021		2031	
	M	F	M	F
0-14	2177.0	2064.7	2267.3	2149.6
15-24	1550.9	1472.1	1576.8	1495.6
25-39	2450.4	2380.5	2535.4	2457.8
40-49	1659.4	1612.7	1737.8	1684.4
50-59	1635.8	1610.6	1659.7	1616.7
60-64	741.3	751.6	800.7	805.2
65-69	620.7	657.6	721.5	750.8
70-74	530.7	578.8	628.1	681.9
75+	702.7	983.5	1021.4	1417.8

can be gained from the population of working age, defined as 15 to 64 years. By 2031, approximately half the people of working age will be between 40 and 64 years old, and almost 30 per cent will be aged 50 or older. The age distribution of the labour force depends also on labour force participation rates, but if these stay constant, then the number of workers over the age of 40 will rise relative to the number of younger workers due to the increased proportion of people over 40 in the working age population. Hence, between 1988 and 2021, the labour force becomes noticeably older. However, most of the ageing occurs between 1988 and 2011, and between 2021 and 2031 the proportion of people of working age who are between 40 and retirement age barely changes.

These data show that the total number of people over the age of 75 increases over time, the most significant rise occurring between 2021 and 2031. However, the number of people over the age of 75 is about 47 per cent of those over 65 in 2031. This proportion actually declines over the period 2001 to 2011. This variation reflects the slow population growth during the 1930s and early 1940s, followed by the post-war baby boom. The proportion of the population over 65 and over 75 will increase more markedly after 2031, resulting in greater repercussions on social expenditures than occur in the period considered in this study.

3.2.2   Social Expenditure Data

Combined Commonwealth and State social expenditure per capita are set out in Tables 3.3 and 3.4, and this forms the matrix S. These figures concentrate on those items of government expenditure which vary with age. Housing outlays, which may vary somewhat with age, are also not included. The age groupings for groups one and two differ slightly from the ABS population groupings in Tables 3.1 and 3.2 above; they are 0-15 and 16-24. These data are from Commonwealth Department of Community Services and Health Policy Development Division (1990). The Commonwealth expenditure totals were taken from Tables 3.2 to 3.5, pp.18-25. Total State spending was taken from CDC (1990, Table 3.7, p.28). Per capita spending was calculated by dividing the sum of total State and Commonwealth expenditure in each category and age group by the total population age distribution for June 1988. Hence, the per capita figures above are slightly different to the per capita figures in CDC (1990) because different population data are used.

The change in relative importance of different types of public spending may cause a change in the mix of Commonwealth-State outlays. State governments have most of the responsibility for education. In 1988, total Commonwealth education outlays were $5551.9 million according to the Commonwealth Department of Community Services and Health Policy Development Division, hereafter referred to as CDC (1990, p.24), whereas State education outlays were $8136 million (CDC, 1990, p.28). However, spending on health and welfare (including assistance to the aged, unemployment benefits, employment programmes and other social security spending) fall mainly under Commonwealth jurisdiction. State health outlays were $6149 million (CDC 1990, p.28) compared to Commonwealth total health outlays of $10024 million (CDC 1990, p.22); total welfare outlays for the States were $867 million (CDC, 1990, p.28), whereas for the Commonwealth they were $22210 million (CDC, 1990, p.19). Therefore, if education spending falls and aged assistance and health outlays rise as a result of the ageing population, Commonwealth social outlays will increase in importance relative to State social outlays, assuming no change in current policies.

Table 3.3: Social Expenditure Costs per Year per Head

Age	Age Pension	Other Aged Assistance	Unemployment Benefits	Other Social Security
0-15	0	3.64	0	882.98
16-24	0.30	1.84	384.46	345.89
25-39	1.12	1.67	300.21	422.62
40-49	6.19	2.78	211.03	502.82
50-59	57.19	5.86	215.20	1087.91
60-64	1138.77	12.15	184.49	1729.03
65-59	2430.04	30.82	0	2041.46
70-74	3368.12	59.93	0	1625.66
75+	4168.33	262.61	0	1134.58

Table 3.4: Social Expenditure Costs per Year per Head

Age	Health	Education	Employment	Total
0-15	443.15	913.00	1.89	2244.66
16-24	443.36	1528.55	165.32	2869.72
25-39	602.43	303.21	59.25	1690.51
40-49	565.05	140.69	37.75	1466.31
50-59	941.80	57.56	24.66	2390.18
60-64	1579.01	24.27	13.39	4681.11
65-69	2185.35	15.57	0	6703.24
70-74	3254.59	16.23	0	8324.53
75+	6110.80	12.38	0	11688.70

The spending breakdown in CDC (1990) was much more detailed for Commonwealth than for State outlays. The information on Commonwealth expenditure included aged pensions, unemployment benefits, social welfare, health, employment and education. State figures, on the other hand, covered only the broad groupings of welfare, health and education. There was no information on State spending on aged care or other aged services, and no information on employment spending by States.

Calculations for the per capita spending figures in Tables 3.3 and Table 3.4 are as follows. The 'age pensions' spending category in Table 3.3 is calculated using the figures for 'age pensions and allowances' in CDC (1990, Table 3.2, p.18). The 'age pensions and allowances' figures are divided by the 1988 population (in millions). Thus, the 'age pensions' figure for age group two in Table 3.3 above is calculated as: 0.83 / 2.7361. The data for 'other aged assistance' in Table 3.3 are taken from CDC (1990, Table 3.2, p.18) and are made up of total 'assistance to the aged' excluding 'age pensions and allowances'. The value for unemployment benefits in Table 3.3 above is taken from 'unemployment benefits', a subheading under 'assistance to unemployed/sick', CDC (1990, Table 3.2, p.19).

Unemployment benefits and aged pensions are not under State jurisdiction, hence, State figures were not relevant in cases (i) and (iii). State outlays specifically on the aged were unavailable, therefore, 'other aged assistance' may underestimate total government spending in this area. Information on 'other social security' includes Commonwealth and State figures. The Commonwealth data are taken from the 'total social security/welfare' figures, CDC (1990, Table 3.2, p.19), but exclude unemployment benefits, and assistance to the aged. The State data are taken from the 'welfare' figures, CDC (1990, Table 3.7, p28). The State and Commonwealth figures in corresponding age groups are added and then divided by the population age distribution for June 1988, $P(1)$. 'other social security' includes State spending on the aged and some State employment outlays.

State Spending

In an attempt to find more information on State spending, total spending in each State in the categories education, employment, health and community services was calculated from the 1988-9 *State Budget Papers* using figures for actual spending in 1987-8. The latter were invariably larger than the State spending per capita data provided in CDC (1990). For example, per capita State spending on health was \$371.835 according to CDC (1990, p.28, Table 3.7), dividing by the population for June 1988 from ABS (1989b), whereas the figure calculated from the *State Budget Papers* 1988-9 was \$571.84 per head, dividing by the same population. The figures for community services and education from CDC (1990) were \$52.43 and \$491.96 per head respectively; however, the corresponding *Budget Paper* figures were \$195.96 and \$615.29 per capita. State employment spending derived from the *Budget Papers* was \$39.82 per head. Employment spending by the State governments was not provided by CDC (1990).

The *State Budget Paper* figures were not used for two reasons. First, each State aggregated spending types in different ways, causing uncertainty as to what types of spending were included under each category heading. Thus there was no consistency of spending categories between States or with the composition of Commonwealth spending. For example, expenditure on youth affairs under the 'community services' heading, may include employment spending in one State, but not in another. In Victoria, the Youth Guarantee programme seemed to include employment spending whereas it was unclear whether expenditure on youth affairs in other States also included employment spending. Another area of uncertainty was State administration costs since a proportion of these was excluded from the Commonwealth figures; see CDC (1990, appendix B, p.B1). Secondly, the *State Budget Papers* did not provide enough information to enable a breakdown of State outlays according to the Commonwealth age groupings provided in CDC (1990). This caused difficulties as to how to account for the different population age structure in each State. Another possible source of information on State spending is the ABS *National Accounts*. However, these also do not give age breakdowns for Commonwealth and State spending and do not provide the expenditure detail required by the present study.

Since the CDC (1990) spending categories for the States would be consistent with the Commonwealth spending categories, and the method for calculating administration costs the same, the CDC (1990) figures seemed preferable. Also, the age groupings were the same for Commonwealth and State data. Unfortunately, CDC (1990) defines the first age group differently from the ABS and other publications. The first age group in the CDC paper is 0-15, whereas the ABS uses 0-14 years old. The difference is due to the definition of a dependant, which the Commonwealth government defines as below 16 years of age. As mentioned in the introduction to this section, data for social expenditure disaggregated by sex were not available.

The data in Table 3.4 on employment costs may underestimate total social spending in this category because data for State spending on employment in CDC (1990) were not included as a separate category. State employment spending not included in State welfare payments is therefore excluded from this study.

The spending category 'other social security' includes Commonwealth assistance to veterans, the handicapped, families, sole parents and widowed people and other welfare payments such as outlays for funerals and temporary accommodation. State welfare payments, which are not broken down into spending types in CDC (1990) are also included. This category of government spending is not obviously age related; for example, assistance for handicapped people is not restricted to a particular age range. However, other social security outlays are higher for the older age groups, reaching a maximum for the 65 - 69 age group. Outlays per head for those aged 50 and over are more than double the payments made per person to those aged between 16 and 49, and are much higher than outlays per head for the 0-16 age group. Tables 3.3 and 3.4 show that public outlays per capita on the age pension and other aged assistance, health and other social security are higher for older age groups, whereas spending per head on unemployment benefits, education and employment programmes are higher for younger people.

Table 3.5: Labour Force

Age	Unemployment		Participation	
Group	M	F	M	F
0-14	0	0	0	0
15-24	12.8	13.4	73.5	65.9
25-39	5.3	6.9	94.6	64.5
40-49	4.2	4.8	93.3	66.3
50-59	4.9	4.5	80.7	41.8
60-64	8.7	1.0	48.7	13.3
65-69	0.4	0	13.4	4.6
70-74	0.6	0	9.3	2.2
75+	0	0	4.4	0.9

3.2.3 Labour Force Data

The age-specific participation and unemployment rates are shown in Table 3.5. These were obtained from unpublished *ABS Labour Force Survey* data for 1988. These data were specially tabulated by the ABS from original published ABS civilian labour force data for June 1988 (ABS, 1988, Table 10, p.24, and Table 24, p.31). The published data are organised into age groupings which do not correspond with the age groups specified in the government spending figures in Table 3.3. The ABS kindly readjusted the age groups to coincide with those used in this study. (The ABS special tabulations used 1988 population data revised in 1992, so their labour force figures are slightly different from those used here, which are not revised.) The first and second age groupings are 0-14 and 15-24, which differ slightly from the age groupings in CDC (1990), but are the same as the ABS population groupings. These data are from Australian Bureau of Statistics Labour Force Survey (unpublished data). Labour Force, unemployment rate and participation rate by sex and by age are based on *1986 Census Benchmarks* (June 1988).

The GDP figure for 1987-8 was obtained from *Australian National Accounts* (ABS 1989-90, Table 2, p.2). This figure was chosen in order to take into account some of the statistical revisions of GDP. The expenditure revalued estimate is used, and is $241,889 million. To calculate productivity, GDP figure was divided by employment as calculated in the model for the base year, 1988. Using benchmark data, the implied total unemployment rate is 0.072, and the labour force is 8,008,159. Employment as calculated by the model was therefore 7,434,829. Hence, GDP per employed person is $32,534.57. These figures from the model can be compared with the actual data for 1988. There were 7,353,400 people employed in 1988 (ABS *Labour Force Statistics,* cat. no. 6101, 1988, p.40, Table 3.2) and the number of people in the civilian labour force was 7,892,100 (ABS cat. no. 6101, 1988, p.15, Table 2.2). These differences in absolute levels are not important for the projections reported below.

3.3 Benchmark Projections

The benchmark projections for 1988, 2001, 2011, 2021 and 2031 focus on the effects of the changing population age structure on social expenditures, holding constant all other factors influencing public expenditure. The increase in the proportion of older people in the population, holding constant participation and unemployment rates and real outlay levels and assuming no changes in government social policy, causes the structure of total public social expenditure to change. The number of recipients for each different government social expenditure programme will rise or fall depending on whether the programme focuses on the old or the young. For example, as the number of people over the age of 65 rises, the number of people claiming the aged pension will increase, causing total public pension payments to increase. However, a concurrent fall in the number of people between the ages of 0 and 24 will reduce the number of recipients for education spending.

Population growth occurs in line with the ABS population projections set out above. Participation rates and unemployment rates in each age group are assumed constant at the 1988 levels shown in Table 3.5 throughout the 43-year projection period. Productivity growth is assumed constant throughout the period at 2 per cent per year. Real per capita outlays are also assumed to increase by 2 per cent per year in each spending category, since if productivity growth is some measure of the rise in the standard of living, then real government spending per head can be expected to rise at the same rate.

Table 3.6: Projected Employment

Year	Number Empl ('000)	Lab Force (Civilian)	U rate	Part rate
1988	7434.829	8008.159	0.072	0.484
2001	9052.507	9709.269	0.068	0.490
2011	9951.123	10666.953	0.067	0.483
2021	10501.475	11250.546	0.067	0.465
2031	10870.573	11640.968	0.068	0.448

3.3.1 Employment and the Labour Force

Employment and the labour force resulting from the changing population applied to constant unemployment and participation rates are shown in Table 3.6. The employment rate rises slightly as the proportion of older people in age groups with lower unemployment rates increases over time. The total participation rate at first rises from 0.484 to 0.490 between 1988 and 2001, but falls thereafter. This is probably driven by both the number of people of working age and the age structure of the workforce. The percentage of the population of working age rises markedly between 1988 and 2001, having a positive effect on the total participation rate. However, although the percentage of the population of working age rises also between 2001 and 2011, more people fall into the 50-59 age group. People aged 50-59 have lower participation rates than those aged 25-49, so the impact on the total participation rate is negative.

The increase in the proportion of older people in the population is associated with a reduction in the percentage of total social spending on unemployment benefits, employment and education, whereas the percentage devoted to aged pensions, other aged assistance and health rises. This is as expected, since spending per capita falls with age in the former social spending categories, but rises in the latter categories. Other social security payments decline as a percentage of total social spending, except for a slight rise between 2001 and 2011. This is perhaps because outlays per person in the other social security category are highest in the 60-64 and 65-69 age ranges which rise markedly between 2001 and 2011.

Table 3.7: Dependency Ratios

Year	Young	Old	Total	Effective
1988	0.496	0.242	0.738	1.22
2001	0.446	0.265	0.711	1.19
2011	0.415	0.299	0.714	1.22
2021	0.404	0.388	0.792	1.30
2031	0.406	0.480	0.887	1.39

Spending on the over-75 age group increases dramatically over time. In 1988, approximately 16 per cent of total social spending was received both by people aged below 15 and those over 75. However, by 2021, the proportion of total outlays spent on those aged 75 and above is approximately double the proportion spent on children under 15. In 2031, people over the age of 75 receive 29.45 per cent of total social spending compared with 10.24 per cent received by people under the age of 15. By 2031, people in the 75 and over age group will be receiving 10.5 per cent of aged pension expenditure and 15.4 per cent of health spending.

Dependency ratios may be used to summarise the burden of different classes of dependants on the working or working-age population. Table 3.7 shows four such ratios. There is a large rise in the old-age dependency ratio, that is, the ratio of the number of people over 65 to the number of people employed. The young dependency ratio, defined as the ratio of 0-15 year olds to the number of people employed, falls. Table 3.7 shows that the total number of dependants (people aged below 15 years and above 65 years) per person employed actually falls from 1988 to 2011, and does not become larger than the 1988 ratio until 2021.

However, the total dependency ratio is a misleading indication of the effects of the ageing population on social expenditures. First, government per capita outlays on those over the age of 65 are higher than outlays on people of 15 or below. Public expenditure on shelter, clothing and food for the elderly occurs in the form of aged assistance, which includes the aged pension. Total Commonwealth spending on assistance to the aged (including pensions) in 1988 was $7,242 million, of which $6,258 million was spent on those over the age of 65 (CDC 1990, p.18, Table 3.2). Government assistance in the area of shelter, clothing and food for young dependants occurs in the form of family allowances. Commonwealth assistance to families was $1,843 million in 1988, all of which was spent on the 0-24 age groups (CDC, 1990, 19, Table 3.2). It has been previously noted that per capita spending on both 'other social security' and 'health' categories was higher for the older age groups than the younger age groups. Referring again to Tables 3.3 and 3.4, total public social spending per head is considerably higher for people over the age of 65 than for young people aged 15 or less. Furthermore, Tables 3.3 and 3.4 illustrate the importance of the over-75 age group in total public spending per head. Secondly, some people over the age of 65 may not rely on the public pension, but may support themselves with superannuation savings. These people may not be classified as dependants. Third, dependent students between the ages of 15 and 64, invalids of working age and the unemployed are also dependent on employed people, but are not counted in the dependency ratios above.

The final column of Table 3.7 shows the 'effective dependency ratio', defined as the difference between the population and employment divided by employment. In 1988, each employed person supported himself or herself plus 1.22 other people, whereas in 2031 each employed person will be supporting an additional 1.39 other people. The reason for the variation is that, although the employment rate increases over time, the proportion of the population of working age is falling, that is, the labour force is contracting, so employment as a percentage of the total population is decreasing; this is also shown in Table 3.7.

3.3.2 Social Expenditure

GDP is projected to increase from $241,889 million in 1988 to $828,715 million in 2031. The effect of population ageing on the social expenditure to GDP ratio is illustrated in Table 3.8, where it can be seen that the greatest increase in the ratio occurs between 2011 and 2031. These increases correspond to the years when the largest percentage rises occur in the over-70 age group. The social expenditure to GDP ratio increases 11.5 per cent between

Table 3.8: Projections of Social Expenditure/GDP

Year	1988	2001	2011	2021	2031
Ratio	0.2036	0.2069	0.219	0.2442	0.2738

2011 and 2021, and 10.8 per cent between 2021 and 2031. The proportion of the population aged over 70 rises by 26 per cent between 2011 and 2021 and by 24 per cent between 2021 and 2031.

The slow rise in the ratio over the period 2001 to 2011 is associated with the property that the proportion of people aged over 75 years actually declines over that period. Population ageing increases more rapidly at the end of the period, giving rise to the increase in the ratio to about 0.27 in 2031. These results are higher than those obtained by Kelley (1988). His baseline projections imply a growth in the ratio of social expenditure to GDP from 0.20 in 1985 to 0.184 in the year 2000, and to 0.218 in 2030. Kelley made the same benchmark assumptions regarding the rates of growth of social expenditure per capita and productivity, namely that all grow at the rate of 0.02 per year.

3.4   Sensitivity Analysis

Sensitivity analysis is undertaken in this section to observe the effect on the social expenditure to GDP ratio of changing the benchmark assumptions. Possible changes to the benchmark assumptions include altering the population projections, immigration projections, fertility rates, mortality rates, labour force participation rates, unemployment rates, real spending growth rates, productivity growth rates and changing government policies which affect any of the above. Since there are so many possibilities, this study will concentrate on the ramifications of changing assumptions about real spending growth, unemployment rates and participation rates. The effect of a change in productivity growth is the easiest change to examine, as shown in section 3.2. For longer periods, such changes can be substantial. For example, if the productivity growth rate is increased from the benchmark case of 0.02 to 0.025, the social expenditure ratio in the year 2031 falls from 0.2731

Table 3.9: Projections for Alternative Expenditure Growth Rates

	1988	2001	2011	2021	2031
Health: 0.025	0.2036	0.2116	0.2281	0.2596	0.2978
Employment: 0.025	0.2036	0.2071	0.2192	0.2447	0.2745

to 0.2219.

3.4.1 Real Public Spending Growth

Heller *et al.* (1986) noted that in the G7 OECD countries health expenditure in the past increased at a greater rate than productivity growth, suggesting that a realistic assumption for future growth in medical costs would be for health costs to exceed the rate of productivity growth by between 0.3 and 0.9 percentage points annually (Heller *et al.* 1986, p.39). In the light of this, the annual growth rate for health spending was changed from the benchmark rate of 0.02 to a rate of 0.025 per year. The resulting change in the social expenditure to GDP ratio is large, as shown in Table 3.9, because health spending is such a large proportion of total social spending. Changing the growth of employment spending by the same amount, also shown in Table 3.9, has a smaller effect on the social expenditure to GDP ratio because expenditure on employment is a very small part of total social spending.

Age pension spending and other age assistance may also grow at a faster rate than productivity growth if the increasing proportion of elderly people in the population utilise their greater political power to fight for higher pensions. Since age pension expenditure is such a large portion of total social spending, any change in government pension policy, such as government superannuation regulation, means-testing, the retirement age and other eligibility provisions, will have a large impact on the social expenditure to GDP ratio.

3.4.2 The Labour Market

In the benchmark projections, although the age-specific unemployment and participation rates are held constant, the total unemployment rate and the total participation rate change over the 43-year period due to the changing population age structure. Specifically, the total number of unemployed people as a percentage of the workforce falls over time as the proportion of people in the older age groups with lower unemployment rates rises. The assumed real growth of 2 per cent per year in total unemployment spending will therefore probably overstate the true per annum growth rate. This is because the benefits for each unemployed person may grow at 2 per cent per year, but the declining number of unemployed recipients will mean that total government unemployment outlays grow at less than 2 per cent.

The expression in equation (3.10) is a closer approximation when all age groups grow at the same rate. However, if the population in each group grows at different rates, the effect of the changing population age structure on public unemployment expenditure is omitted. The same factors affecting unemployment outlays probably indirectly affect public employment spending as well, if the level of employment spending is related to the number of people unemployed.

Using equation (3.10), the effect of the change in the total unemployment rate and participation rate due to the changing population age structure on the growth of public unemployment spending can be approximated. Holding the real growth of unemployment benefits received by each unemployed person constant at 2 per cent per annum, growth in total unemployment expenditure over the 43-year period is 1.6 per cent per year. This causes the social expenditure to GDP ratio in 2031 to change from 0.2738 to 0.2718.

3.4.3   Unemployment Rates

It is very difficult to predict age-specific unemployment rates for long periods into the future. In order, therefore, to consider how sensitive the social expenditure to GDP ratio is to changes in unemployment rates, arbitrary alterations were made to the total unemployment rate which were assumed to apply equally across all age groups.

As stated above, although the unemployment rates in each age group are held constant in the benchmark case, the total unemployment rate falls from 0.072 in 1988 to 0.066 in 2031, due to the changing population age structure. It was therefore decided to observe the opposite case of a rise in the overall unemployment rate, taking into account the resultant growth in total unemployment spending. However, to calculate a constant growth rate per annum for unemployment expenditure over the entire period, equation (3.10) requires constant growth each year in the participation rate. Growth per year in the overall participation rate is not constant over the 43 year period due to the changing population age structure. Hence, a long-term view will be taken using the participation rates in 1988 and 2031, assuming a constant growth rate per annum in participation in between, and therefore ignoring the social expenditure to GDP ratio in interim years. A short-term view from 1988 to 2001 will also be taken.

To estimate the effect of an increase in the unemployment rate from 0.072 in 1988 to 0.11 in 2001, an approximate growth rate per year in total public unemployment spending was calculated using equation 3.10 to be 0.055. The unemployment rate in each age group was increased by 52 per cent, in line with the 52 per cent increase in the total unemployment rate from 0.072 to 0.11. As explained above, this method does not take into account the change in the population age structure, so the figures are approximate, and the total unemployment rate will not be exactly 0.11 in 2001 (in fact it is 0.103 per cent). These alterations cause the social expenditure to GDP ratio in 2001 to be 0.2222, instead of 0.2069 as in the benchmark projections.

To observe such a change over a longer period of time, the unemployment rate was assumed to rise at a constant rate per annum to 0.11 by 2031, so the unemployment rate in each age group was increased by 0.0099 per year. Total unemployment spending per capita was calculated according to equation (3.10) to grow at approximately 2.82 per cent per year. This caused the social expenditure to GDP ratio in 2031 to rise to 0.2898 from 0.2738 in the benchmark case.

3.4.4 Labour Force Participation Rates

In addition to the benchmark participation rates shown in Table 3.5, assumed to be constant over the whole period, several other projections are available.

Table 3.10: Alternative Population Projections

Year	1988	2001	2011	2021	2031
Series C	0.2036	0.2059	0.2071	0.2438	0.2757
Series D	0.2036	0.2066	0.2200	0.2496	0.2853

Four other sets of participation rate projections are available. These include two sets developed by the Department of Employment Education and Training (DEET, 1991, p.133), the ABS (1992b) for the year 2001, and the projections of the Centre for International Economics (CIE, 1988, p.37) for each of the census years. These alternative projections assume slightly lower participation rates for males and higher rates for females (up to retirement age). However, they have very little effect on the projected social expenditure to GDP ratios and are therefore not reported here.

3.4.5   Changing Demographic Assumptions

The alternative ABS population projections provided in ABS (1989a) were used to replace the population projections in Tables 3.1 and 3.2 as a starting point for examining the influence of demographic assumptions on the social expenditure to GDP ratio. Series C, ABS (1989), assumes a different fertility rate to the population projections outlined in Tables 3.1 and 3.3, but the same immigration, whereas series D, ABS (1989) changes both the fertility rate and the immigration rate. Series C, ABS (1989), assumes a constant fertility rate of 1.66 children per woman and annual net migration of 125,000 people per year. Series D, ABS (1989), assumes a fertility rate of 1.66 children per woman and net migration of 125,000 people per year until 1994, followed by a decline in migration to 80,000 per annum in the year 2000, remaining constant at 80,000 thereafter. Series D thus implies a greater degree of ageing. The effect on the social expenditure to GDP ratio of replacing the benchmark population projections with these different projections is illustrated in Table 3.10.

The sensitivity analyses so far considered have involved changes in just one component of the framework at a time, and they have produced relatively

Table 3.11: Optimistic and Pessimistic Assumptions

Year	2001	2011	2021	2031
Optimistic	0.193	0.197	0.216	0.231
Pessimistic	0.219	0.239	0.276	0.320

small variations in the ratio of social expenditure to GDP. The following subsection examines two cases involving several simultaneous changes.

3.4.6 Two Variations

The range of possible sensitivity analyses is obviously extensive, but it was decided to examine two variations on the benchmark case. In the 'optimistic' case the growth rate of productivity was increased to 0.022 while the growth rates of per capita expenditure on pensions, other aged assistance and health were reduced to 0.18. Furthermore, from 2001 the male unemployment rates in the three age groups 16-24, 25-39 and 40-49 were reduced to 0.11, 0.05 and 0.04 respectively, while for females the corresponding rates were reduced to 0.12, 0.05 and 0.04. These may be compared with the benchmark rates of Table 3.8. The participation rates in the 60-64 age group were increased to 0.55 and 0.25 for males and females respectively.

For the 'pessimistic' case the growth rate of productivity was reduced to 0.018 while the growth rates of per capita spending were increased to 0.022 for the pension, other aged assistance and health categories. The unemployment rates from 2001 for the age group 16-24 were increased to 0.14 for both males and females, and for the age group 25-39 they were increased to 0.06 and 0.07 respectively for males and females. Labour force participation in the 60-64 year age group was reduced to 0.4 and 0.1 for males and females respectively.

In the pessimistic case, the (endogenous) aggregate unemployment rate drops only to 7 per cent in the year 2031, from 7.2 per cent in 1988 (the slight fall, despite the increase in several age specific rates, arises of course because of the population ageing and the fact that age-specific rates are lower in older age groups). In the optimistic case the aggregate unemployment rate falls to 5.8 per cent. The aggregate participation rate falls from 48.4 per cent in 1988 to 44 per cent in the pessimistic case and to 46 per cent in the optimistic case, by the year 2031.

The social expenditure ratios for these two cases are shown in Table 3.11. The differences between the two situations are not dramatic in terms of the assumptions underlying the projections, yet the difference in the social expenditure ratios is 9 percentage points by 2031. Such a difference is large in terms of the revenue requirements of the government. The role of the assumed productivity growth is perhaps worth isolating, as it contributes approximately half of the difference between the ratios for the two variations. If only productivity growth were changed from the benchmark case, values of 0.018 and 0.022 would produce ratios of 0.2979 and 0.2517 in 2031.

3.5   Conclusions

Projections of the social expenditure to GDP ratio have been used by governments to aid policy decisions in such areas as immigration and superannuation. This study has shown that the social expenditure to GDP ratio is heavily dependent on assumptions made about real spending growth, productivity growth, unemployment and participation rates. The framework makes clear the assumptions underlying the projections and enables the results of changing the assumptions to be easily compared.

The benchmark projections of the social expenditure to GDP ratio assume constant age distributions of unemployment and participation rates, constant real spending and productivity growth and population projections produced by the ABS. According to these assumptions, the social expenditure to GDP ratios rise markedly only after 2011. The ABS population projections (ABS 1989a) suggest that, as a result of population ageing, the ratio will rise even more after 2031. The projected ratios are higher than those obtained by earlier studies.

Sensitivity analysis illustrated that altering the benchmark assumptions regarding real expenditure growth, productivity growth and unemployment and participation rates caused significant changes in the social expenditure to GDP ratio.

It should be stressed that projections of this kind provide only a partial view of the types of problem that may be faced by policy makers. They illustrate only the orders of magnitude of expenditure requirements which result from demographic and other changes. A more complete analysis would require the detailed treatment of revenue considerations. Population ageing has implications for the tax base, so that tax *rates* will not necessarily have to follow the expenditure ratios.

The demographic projections used here depend significantly on assumed migration flows, as well as fertility and survival rates. In view of the importance of migration in the Australian context, this aspect is examined in the following chapter.

Chapter 4

Migration and Population Ageing

This chapter concentrates on the implications for population ageing of immigration. Most studies of the impact of immigration focus on the role of alternative immigration levels, and do not consider the impact of changing the composition of the net intake, that is, differentiating between the country of birth of migrants and the demographic and social characteristics associated with it. This is true of projections such as those of the ABS (1989b), the BIPR (1992), the National Population Council (1991, 1992) and the EPAC (1988, 1994). The present chapter extends the analysis of the impact of migration by considering the differences associated with birthplace, particularly differences in mortality and fertility rates. For an extensive treatment of immigration, including the effects on social expenditure, see Alvarado and Creedy (1997).

The basic framework required for projecting population, allowing for migration is described in chapter 2. Section 4.1 describes this framework and presents the benchmark projections using that framework. Section 4.2 presents the main demographic differences among the Australian resident population according to country of birth. Section 4.3 studies the impact of these differences on population growth and age structure.

4.1   Benchmark Projections

The number of people in a country at the beginning of a year is made up
of people who lived in the country at the start of the previous year and
who neither died nor migrated to other countries during that year, plus the
number of surviving people who migrated from other countries during that
year, plus the births during the previous year. The flows can be represented
in a social accounting framework which enables projections to be made. The
framework used to produce the projections is described in detail in chapter 2.
Such population projections require a large number of assumptions regarding
birth, death and migration rates for males and females in each age group,
along with the way in which these rates are assumed to change over time. A
simplifying assumption commonly made is that all migrants, once they arrive
in the country, immediately acquire a common set of fertility and mortality
characteristics so that the composition of the population can be ignored. The
major aim of the present chapter is to modify this type of assumption, but
for comparison purposes a 'benchmark' set of projections is presented which
follows the standard approach.

Assuming annual net migration of 125,000 persons, fertility rates constant at the 1990 level, and mortality falling as described by the long-term
rates of annual change estimated by the ABS (1989b, p.27), the benchmark
population projections are shown in Tables 4.1 and 4.2.

The results are grouped into nine age groups, corresponding to those
used by the ABS. These projections show that although Australia has one
of the youngest and fastest growing populations of the Western countries,
it is expected to grow older during the next few decades. The proportion
of people younger than 40 years of age falls from 62 per cent in 1990 to 49
per cent in 2031, while those aged 65 and over increases from 11 to 20 per
cent during the same period. Population ageing accelerates particularly after
2011. Thus, the proportion of people aged 65 and over increases 27 per cent
between 1990 and 2011, and 43 per cent during the following 20 years. The
ageing increases to the point that the proportion of middle-aged people also
starts to fall. Although the number of people between 40 and 64 years of

Table 4.1: Population Projections: 1990-2011

Age	1990 M	1990 F	2001 M	2001 F	2011 M	2011 F
1-14	1917.8	1823.8	1975.4	1896.1	2022.2	1944.0
15-24	1413.8	1353.6	1370.1	1314.4	1503.1	1452.0
25-39	2080.0	2052.6	2248.9	2191.0	2231.2	2173.4
40-49	1154.0	1102.1	1458.4	1447.2	1590.0	1557.8
50-59	788.3	758.5	1206.9	1185.2	1435.5	1441.6
60-64	366.5	369.0	416.5	414.2	608.4	627.6
65-69	314.9	351.1	332.0	348.7	488.4	509.3
70-74	216.4	270.0	289.0	322.3	335.6	370.3
75-99	279.9	473.0	453.9	711.8	534.2	812.4
All ages	8531.7	8553.7	9751.1	9830.9	10748.6	10888.4

Table 4.2: Population Projections: 2021-2031

Age	2021 M	2021 F	2031 M	2031 F
1-14	2100.9	2018.7	2222.5	2135.0
15-24	1546.6	1496.7	1586.3	1533.8
25-39	2385.0	2335.5	2492.2	2447.5
40-49	1554.5	1517.2	1646.7	1612.9
50-59	1569.2	1552.1	1539.9	1514.2
60-64	714.6	735.2	775.4	784.9
65-69	597.4	646.7	668.4	705.4
70-74	497.4	562.3	593.8	661.7
75-99	716.4	1032.1	996.7	1443.5
All ages	11682.0	11896.5	12521.9	12838.9

age increases from 27 to 34 per cent of the total population between 1990 and 2011, it falls to 31 per cent by 2031. Similarly, whereas the number of people younger than 40 rises 17 per cent between 1990 and 2031, that of people aged 75 and over increases by more than 200 per cent during the same period. These trends can be explained by the combined effect of the assumed decline in mortality rates and the 'baby boom' generation entering retirement after 2011.

4.1.1   Data Sources

The population projection model requires the age distributions to be given by single years of age. Whenever the data were not available in this form, the total number included in each age group was divided by the number of years in the age group and the same value was assigned to each age within the group. The base year is 1990, but in some cases the average of the years 1988-90 appeared to be more appropriate.

The estimated resident population of Australia by sex and single year of age at 30 June 1990 is given in 'Estimated Resident Population by Sex and Age, States and Territories of Australia', (ABS Cat. no. 3201.0, Table 1, pp.3-6, 1991).

Emigration data are given by the average 1988-90 age and sex distribution of permanent departures, in 'Overseas Arrivals and Departures, Australia', (ABS Cat. no. 3404.0, Table 10, p.14, 1991).

Mortality data are taken from the *Australian Life Tables* 1985-87, estimated by the Office of the Australian Government Actuary (1991). Multiplying the probability of a person of a given age dying within a year by the resident population gives the number of deaths for the initial year by sex and single year of age. Subtracting from the resident population the number of deaths and emigrants and dividing by resident population gives the survival rates. These survival rates change over time with decreasing mortality rates. The long-term rates of annual change in age-specific death rates estimated by the ABS (1989b, Table 4.10, p.27) were used.

The average 1988-90 permanent overseas arrivals (immigrants) by sex and age were taken from 'Overseas Arrivals and Departures, Australia', (ABS Cat. no. 3404.0, Table 9, p.13, 1991). New settlers are younger than people emigrating from Australia. Similarly, while 38 per cent of the total population in 1990 were younger than 25 years of age, 45 per cent of new arrivals were in this age group.

Age-specific birth rates are taken from 'Births Australia', ABS Cat. no. 3301.0, Table 4, p.5 (1991a). Fertility rates in Australia are still higher than in most developed countries, and in recent years the total fertility rate experienced a slight increase from 1.84 in 1989 to 1.90 in 1990. The highest number of births is concentrated in the 25-29 age range, followed by the 30-34 age group. Hence, most of the 'baby boom' generation has not yet passed the peak childbearing ages, which guarantees high levels of natural increase of the population during the early and mid-1990s; see NPC (1991 and 1992) and BIPR (1992). For women younger than 15 and older than 49 years, a zero fertility rate was assumed.

The average 1988-90 proportion of total births that are male was 0.51, given in 'Births Australia' (ABS Cat. no. 3301.0, Table 2 , p.4, 1991a).

4.1.2 Population Decomposition

The majority of migrants arrive in Australia as adults, so their social and demographic characteristics differ from those of people born in Australia. But the above projections assume that immigrants and persons born in Australia do not differ significantly in terms of fertility and mortality. The appropriateness of this assumption is discussed in the present section.

It is reasonable to expect that people from different countries display different characteristics. These differences range from demographic factors such as fertility and mortality rates to economic variables such as unemployment and participation rates, although this chapter focuses on the most relevant demographic characteristics. If the fertility of immigrants is substantially higher than that of females born in Australia, population ageing could be offset by immigration.

For many years the source of migrants was mainly Europe, particularly the UK and Ireland. Since the 1970s, ethnic diversity and therefore a wider variety of social and cultural backgrounds has been one of the main characteristics of migration. Similarly, these changes have been accompanied by a greater variety in entry categories as well as changes in the relative importance of each of these categories over time. In general, over the last two to three decades there has been a decline in the relative importance of skilled and unsponsored migrants in favour of family migration and to a lesser extent refugees. This has exerted an important effect on the age structure and status of migrants.

4.1.3   Age Structure

Wooden (1990) showed that the proportion of migrants sponsored by families increased from an average of about 30 per cent of adult migrants during the 1960s and 1970s to almost 45 per cent by 1986-7. Of those, 30 per cent were older than 54 years of age. These trends, together with the fact that the large intakes of migrants in the immediate post-war years have already reached retirement age, have resulted in a rapid ageing of the migrant population. Thus, in 1986 the median age of overseas-born persons was 40.7 years compared with 27.5 years for persons born in Australia. There are even larger differences between migrant groups by region and country of origin; for instance, the median age of people born in Europe was 45.2 years, and of those born in the USSR was 62.6 years (ABS 1989d). In 1989, 40 per cent of persons born in Australia were older than 34 years of age while 64 per cent of those born overseas were in that age group; see ABS (1990).

4.1.4   Fertility

There are significant demographic differences between those born in Australia and those born overseas in terms of fertility rates. Table 4.3, from Hugo (1992, p.49), shows that women born overseas, particularly those from non-English-speaking backgrounds (NESB), experience higher fertility rates in each age group than females born in Australia. According to the 1986 census, women from NESB had a total fertility rate almost 11 per cent higher

Table 4.3: Birth Rates by Birthplace of Mother: 1986

Birthplace	Age of mother							TFR
	15-19	20-24	25-29	30-34	35-39	40-44	45-49	
Australia	22.1	93.0	149.0	90.9	25.8	3.9	0.2	1,925
Overseas	24.6	101.9	144.8	96.5	33.7	5.9	0.3	2,039
Total	22.2	93.3	145.8	90.9	27.8	4.4	0.2	1,923
ESB	25.2	93.7	138.2	95.2	29.5	5.0	0.2	1,935
NESB	24.1	110.6	151.1	97.5	36.5	6.5	0.4	2,134

Table 4.4: Death Rates by Birthplace: 1986

Birth place	0-14	15-24	25-34	35-44	45-54	55-64	65-74	75+	Total
Males									
Austr.	1.0	1.4	1.4	2.0	5.5	15.4	38.0	106.2	45195
Overs.	0.4	1.1	1.3	1.6	4.1	13.1	35.2	100.8	16404
ESB	0.3	1.4	1.4	1.7	4.3	14.5	36.3	106.1	8745
NESB	0.4	0.9	1.2	1.5	3.9	12.2	34.2	92.9	7657
Total	1.0	1.3	1.4	1.9	4.9	14.6	36.7	101.9	62195
Females									
Austr.	0.8	0.5	0.6	1.1	3.1	7.8	20.6	80.2	40459
Overs.	0.3	0.4	0.5	0.9	2.5	6.8	19.0	74.5	11905
ESB	0.2	0.4	0.5	0.9	2.8	7.6	19.6	81.1	7252
NESB	0.3	0.4	0.5	0.9	2.2	6.2	18.2	63.1	4650
Total	0.7	0.5	0.5	1.0	2.9	7.5	20.0	76.6	52769

than females born in Australia, and 10.3 per cent above that experienced by women migrating from English speaking backgrounds (ESB). Among the more fertile ethnic groups were those coming from the Middle East and Asian countries. Thus, for example, 45 per cent of Lebanese, 40 per cent of Arab, 31 per cent of Khmer and 27 per cent of Laos women had four or more children ; see Kee (1992, p.6).

4.1.5 Mortality

People born overseas have mortality rates lower than those born in Australia. Table 4.4 shows that NESB migrants have the lowest rates. These mortality rates are much higher than those given in the Australian life tables that were used to obtain the benchmark population projections discussed in section 4.1.

Tables 4.3 and 4.4 show that those born overseas and in Australia are heterogeneous groups, and Kee (1992) has shown that these characteristics persist for several generations. Therefore it seems desirable to incorporate some allowance for these differences in projections. Although the heterogeneity between those born in Australia and those born overseas is quite clear, the characteristics of ESB migrants are much closer to the group of those born in Australia than to those of NESB migrants. This is even more evident when social and economic aspects are taken into account. Hence, it seems appropriate to redefine the Australian resident population as made up of just two groups: those born in Australia and in other English-speaking countries and their descendants on the one hand, referred to as AESB, and NESB migrants and their descendants on the other hand. This population decomposition is used in the next section.

4.2   Alternative Projections

The population projections in section 4.1 were made under the assumption that, although overseas migration played a role in determining the size and growth of the Australian population, the only difference added by migrants was in terms of age and sex distribution. But the above discussion showed that those born in Australia and those born overseas, and particularly the NESB migrants, are quite heterogeneous. Hence, this section examines the effect on the population structure of changing the benchmark assumptions. Thus, while the benchmark framework assumed the extreme case of homogeneity, the other extreme, whereby the NESB migrants are treated as being a separate group from that of AESB people, is now assumed. The Australian resident population is thus made up of two main groups: Australian combined with ESB migrants and their descendants, giving AESB, and migrants from non-English-speaking backgrounds (NESB) and their descendants. The fertility and mortality rates of those born in Australia are assigned to both Australian and ESB migrants.

Data availability is a severe constraint given the high level of disaggregation required. Most of the data are from the Census of 1986, while other data required the processing of unpublished data made available by the Bureau of Immigration and Population Research (BIPR).

4.2.1   Settler Arrivals

During the last five years, settler arrivals from both English and non-English speaking countries have reduced steadily, but while the former have shrunk to almost one-third of the 1988 level, the latter have fallen only by 36 per cent. It is estimated that in 1959 the proportion of NESB migrants first exceeded that of ESB migrants (BIPR, 1991, p.vii), and the gap has increased since then.

Table 4.5 shows the annual average of settler arrivals between 1988-9 and 1992-3 by country of birth and age groups. NESB arrivals are more than double those from English-speaking countries. Both groups have a similar age structure, but again NESB migrants are slightly more concentrated in the middle-aged group while ESB persons are a bit older.

4.2.2   Permanent Departures

While settler arrivals have been decreasing, out migration has increased, though not steadily. Out migration of AESB people reached its peak in 1990-1. The annual average of permanent departures during the last five years are presented in Table 4.6. Almost four times more AESB people left the country compared to NESB people. But 40 per cent of AESB persons leaving the country were born in Australia. There are also significant differences in age structure between emigrants born in English-speaking countries and NESB countries. The proportion of AESB persons younger than 20 years emigrating from Australia was twice that of NESB persons. On the other hand, while 22 per cent of emigrants born in English-speaking countries were older than 39, 40 per cent of NESB leaving Australia fell into that age group.

The differences in number and age structure between arrivals and departures and between ESB and NESB persons define the net migration gain.

Table 4.5: Settler Arrivals: Average 1988-9 to 1992-3

	ESB		NESB	
	M	F	M	F
0-4	2298	2148	3886	3722
5-9	1731	1632	3663	3460
10-14	1283	1211	3086	2849
15-19	1154	1130	2594	3083
20-24	1735	1819	2987	4298
25-29	2969	2965	5243	6272
30-34	2423	2172	5529	5654
35-39	1710	1437	3939	3749
40-44	1184	904	2466	2224
45-49	570	475	1242	1159
50-54	366	334	833	970
55-59	290	323	726	932
60-64	286	387	680	815
65+	664	811	879	1018
Total	18663	17749	37753	40205

Table 4.6: Permanent Departures by Country of Birth: Average 1988-9 to 1992-3

	ESB		NESB	
	M	F	M	F
0-4	1446	1372	94	97
5-9	879	831	114	119
10-14	667	665	127	134
15-19	527	594	111	131
20-24	849	1223	168	235
25-29	1426	1772	312	345
30-34	1385	1426	374	361
35-39	1022	946	345	317
40-44	787	679	307	241
45-49	502	446	228	173
50-54	336	281	181	127
55-59	235	191	133	115
60-64	177	194	124	132
65+	418	507	271	268
Total	10655	11126	2889	2794

Thus, excluding emigrants born in Australia, there was an annual average migration gain of 95,593 people during the last five years. Of those, almost 25 per cent were born in English-speaking countries (other than Australia). That is, net migration gain is almost three times higher for NESB than for ESB people. Comparison of Tables 4.5 and 4.6 shows that the age distribution of ESB arrivals is very similar to that of departures. However, the averge age of NESB departures is substantially higher than that of NESB arrivals, so that the absolute levels of the flows have an effect on population ageing.

The rest of the assumptions required, including the annual decline in mortality rates and the proportion of births that are male, are the same as those used to make the benchmark projections in section 4.1. These assumptions are applied to both population groups, AESB and NESB persons.

4.2.3   Population Projections

The method used to project population under the new assumptions is to take each population group, AESB and NESB persons, with its corresponding set of data. Then, applying the population model, projections are made for each group as if they were two separate populations. Finally, the two groups are added together for each year of the projection period to obtain projections for the total Australian population.

This method assumes that each population group keeps its demographic characteristics constant during the projection period, and that they develop independently of each other so that later generations absorb the characteristics of the group in which they are born. In the case of NESB, second and later generations throughout the projection period are, obviously, born in Australia, but for present purposes they are referred to as NESB persons.

Tables 4.7 and 4.8 present the new set of projections, using the same assumptions employed to make the benchmark projections, that is, an annual net migration of 125000 persons, fertility rates constant, and mortality falling as described by the long-term rates of annual change estimated by the ABS. Given that during the last five years, 75 per cent of the migration gain

Table 4.7: Population Projections: 2001-2011

Age	2001 M	2001 F	2011 M	2011 F
1-14	1918.96	1843.45	1997.09	1918.07
15-24	1325.77	1274.23	1440.26	1393.66
25-39	2121.77	2103.18	2149.40	2116.58
40-49	1279.24	1271.58	1508.00	1505.42
50-59	992.25	991.17	1257.62	1267.61
60-64	449.12	468.16	473.29	490.62
65-69	414.63	448.41	420.42	455.35
70-74	278.00	325.67	355.07	410.43
75-99	344.10	511.00	552.21	789.57
All Ages	9123.84	9236.85	10153.36	10347.31

corresponded to NESB persons and 25 per cent to ESB persons, the net intake of 125,000 is divided into those proportions, and each population group projected under this assumption.

Comparing the results in Table 4.7 and 4.8 with the benchmark projections of Table 4.1 and 4.2 it is found that the figures under the new assumptions are lower than the benchmark. The most significant differences appear in the older age groups, though the gap becomes smaller as the projection period is extended. The total population is 4 per cent lower than the benchmark in 2031. One of the reasons for the lower population figures is that mortality rates used in the new assumption are higher than in the benchmark case. Also, the initial population of 1986 does not include almost a quarter of a million people born at sea and whose country of birth could not be determined. That fact, together with the high levels of immigration particularly during the second half of the 1980s, results in a base population for 1990 of 11.3 per cent lower than the one used to make the benchmark projections.

Alternative projections were based on the benchmark mortality, by applying those rates to the AESB group. From the mortality rates shown in Table 4.4 the ratio of NESB persons to total mortality was taken to estimate corresponding rates for the NESB people. Since these mortality rates were

Table 4.8: Population Projections: 2021-2031

Age	2021		2031	
	M	F	M	F
1-14	2101.58	2018.13	2240.02	2150.88
15-24	1503.71	1453.99	1566.96	1514.07
25-39	2285.54	2258.36	2420.92	2391.83
40-49	1517.51	1498.10	1584.05	1567.72
50-59	1483.48	1497.48	1498.96	1492.80
60-64	655.52	687.36	715.30	737.61
65-69	488.15	523.77	639.12	691.51
70-74	381.73	432.78	537.11	608.37
75-99	710.18	1039.80	850.74	1233.29
All Ages	11127.40	11409.77	12053.18	12388.08

Table 4.9: Age Structures: Two Cases

Age	2001		2011		2021		2031	
	A	B	A	B	A	B	A	B
1-39	0.577	0.577	0.537	0.537	0.515	0.516	0.500	0.504
40-64	0.296	0.297	0.317	0.317	0.326	0.326	0.313	0.310
65-99	0.127	0.126	0.146	0.145	0.159	0.159	0.188	0.186
75-99	0.047	0.046	0.066	0.065	0.079	0.077	0.086	0.085
Total	18308	18379	20365	20547	22292	22619	24046	24574

lower, the population estimates obtained were on average 1 per cent higher than those shown in Table 4.6.

4.2.4 Changing the Level and Composition of Overseas Migration

Changing the level of overseas migration exerts a significant impact on the size and age structure of the population, but the effect is insignificant when only the composition of the intake is modified. Table 4.9 shows the age structure and size of the Australian population assuming a net migration of 125,000 but under two alternative cases. Case A has an intake of 125,000 ESB people and no NESB persons, and Case B has, 125,000 NESB migrants and no ESB migrants.

Table 4.10: Projections of NESB Population

Age	2001 A	2001 B	2011 A	2011 B	2021 A	2021 B	2031 A	2031 B
1-39	0.34	0.54	0.31	0.54	0.38	0.56	0.41	0.55
40-64	0.44	0.35	0.37	0.33	0.23	0.31	0.19	0.29
65-99	0.22	0.12	0.32	0.13	0.40	0.14	0.40	0.15
75-99	0.08	0.04	0.15	0.05	0.21	0.06	0.26	0.07

Case B produces a slightly younger and bigger population. The widest gap between the two cases occurs in 2031 and for the youngest age group, but even then the difference is insignificant, reaching less than 1 per cent. Similarly, total population under Case B in 2031 is only 2 per cent higher than under Case A.

However, the composition of the intake of overseas immigrants does play a role in the ethnic structure of the population. Under case A, NESB persons would shrink to just 5.2 per cent of the Australian population in 2031, from a base year level of 11.3 per cent, whereas under case B, NESB persons would jump to 36.5 per cent of the total population by the last year of the projection period. Similarly, the age structure of the NESB population is significantly affected.

Increasing the net intake of migrants reduces significantly the proportion of elderly people throughout the projection period. Table 4.11 shows the impact of changing the level of immigration on the proportion of people aged 65 and over. The intake is raised assuming 25 per cent of migrants are ESB migrants, and the rest are NESB migrants. The impact increases with time. Thus, by 2031 an intake of 80,000 immigrants reduces the proportion of elderly people by 11 per cent compared with the case were no migration is allowed; it falls by 15 per cent with an immigration of 125,000; and with 170,000 immigrants the proportion of people aged 65 and over decreases by 19 per cent in 2031 compared with a zero migration assumption. Similarly, compared with a zero migration case, total population increases substantially: in 2031 Australian population might be 29 per cent higher with an immigration of 80,000; 45 per cent higher with 125,000 immigrants; and 61

Table 4.11: Changing Immigration and Population Ageing

Immigration	2001	2011	2021	2031
0	0.1382	0.1678	0.1868	0.2199
80,000	0.1303	0.1525	0.1670	0.1959
125,000	0.1265	0.1455	0.1587	0.1866
170,000	0.1229	0.1394	0.1517	0.1792

per cent bigger if net immigration reaches 170,000 annually.

4.2.5   Immigration versus Fertility

Immigration may be regarded as a substitute for fertility; the ageing and size of the population resulting from low fertility rates can be compensated to a certain extent by higher levels of immigration. The question arises of whether fertility is in any sense more 'efficient' in retarding the population ageing process than migration. This question is examined here by considering alternative cases and comparing results with those of Young (1990).

Using the population model employed to produce the benchmark estimates and assuming mortality decline up to the year 2020, as described by the long-term rates of annual change estimated by the ABS (1989b), and a continuation of the 1985-6 age structure of migrants, projections of the population size and age structure since 1986 are made under three alternative cases. Case A assumes a total fertility rate (TFR) of 1.44 and a zero migration intake; case B keeps the level of migration at zero but increases TFR up to 1.85; and case C increases the intake of immigrants to 150,000 per year while keeping the TFR to the original level of 1.44. The results are presented in Table 4.12.

Increasing either the fertility rates or the migrant intake produces the same effect on the proportion of people aged 65 years and over by the end of the projection period. However, higher fertility rates produce a smaller population size and an age pyramid broader at the base than with high levels of immigration. These results are similar to those obtained by Young (1990 p.20) who concludes that 'increasing the level of fertility is a more efficient way of retarding the ageing of the population than increasing the level of

Table 4.12: Variations in Fertility and Immigration

	1-14			65+			Total (000s)		
	A	B	C	A	B	C	A	B	C
2001	15.2	18.7	16.2	14.3	13.7	13.0	16,617	17,340	19,045.3
2011	14.0	17.0	15.3	17.3	16.1	14.9	16,581	17,808	20,818.2
2021	12.2	15.9	14.0	22.9	20.5	18.7	16,085	17,989	22,237.9
2031	11.0	15.4	13.1	28.2	24.0	22.4	15,112	17,791	23,198.4
2046	10.4	15.0	12.7	33.5	25.7	25.6	12,833	16,711	23,651.1

immigration, because the same effect on the proportion aged 65 years or more would be achieved through a smaller increase in population'.

However, it is important to note that immigration appears to slow down the process of ageing faster than do higher fertility rates. While higher fertility reduces the proportion of elderly people by 1.2 percentage points in 2011, high immigration levels decrease that proportion by 2.4 percentage points. Similarly, in 2021 and 2031 high immigration levels reduce the proportion of elderly people by almost 2 percentage points more than high fertility rates; see Table 4.12.

Additional gains in retarding the ageing of the population are achieved when account is taken of the demographic differences between AESB and NESB persons. On the other hand, although immigration produces a lower percentage of people in the youngest age group, it also generates a higher proportion of working-age persons, which could potentially lead to lower dependency ratios.

To illustrate the role of immigration further, Table 4.13 presents additional estimates of the proportion aged 65 and over, using the benchmark model. Whereas with 50,000 immigrants the proportion of elderly people reaches 23.6 per cent by 2040, with 100,000 immigrants or more that proportion can only be reached after several centuries have elapsed. Similarly, with immigration of 150,000, the proportion of elderly people reaches 22.1 per cent by the year 2160, whereas that proportion is reached at the earlier year of 2031 when the intake is reduced to 50,000 immigrants per year.

Table 4.13: Variations in Fertility and Immigration

	50,000			100,000			150,000		
	65+	Total	% 65+	65+	Total	% 65+	65+	Total	% 65+
2001	2411	18172	13	2448	19004	13	2484	19836	13
2011	2950	19285	15	3028	20762	15	3106	22238	14
2021	3841	20160	19	4002	22350	18	4163	24531	17
2031	4577	20714	22	4891	23637	21	5204	26560	20
2046	4880	20753	24	5465	24795	22	6050	28836	21
2081	4699	20069	23	5884	26504	22	7070	32940	22
2160	4395	18823	23	6678	29641	23	8962	40459	22

4.3 Conclusions

On the basis of census data which show that the fertility and mortality characteristics of overseas migrants do not adjust immediately but take several generations, this chapter has extended traditional analyses of migration by proposing a decomposition of the Australian population. This decomposition makes it possible to study the impact on population structure of changing not only the level but also the composition of the migration intake.

The analysis showed that although the composition of immigrants does play a role in determining the ethnic structure of the population, it is the level of immigration that exerts the most significant impact on the size and age structure of the population. Increasing the number of migrants reduces significantly the proportion of elderly people throughout the projection period. For example, with an annual intake of 170,000 immigrants the proportion of people aged 65 and over decreases by 19 per cent and the size of the population rises by 60 per cent by 2031 compared with a zero immigration assumption. The role of immigration in relation to fertility was also contrasted.

Part III

Economic Models and Pensions

Chapter 5

Policy Trade-offs and Pension Systems

Government pensions are typically financed on a pay-as-you-go basis. The debate regarding pension finance and population ageing is often conducted in simple terms of an aged dependency ratio, a replacement ratio (of the pension in relation to average earnings) and the required proportional tax rate to be imposed on the working population. However, such a framework ignores the variation in the types of pension scheme available. For example, countries differ in the extent to which pensions are taxable and means-tested, and some countries rely on revenue from a single source, such as income taxation, while others obtain additional revenue from payroll taxes or social insurance contributions, and consumption taxes. The precise relationship between pension levels and tax rates depends on the details of the schemes as well as on the income distributions of workers and pensions.

The role of dependency ratios is more complex than is usually suggested and it is too simple to think of the policy trade-off only in terms of reducing the pension in order to avoid a rise in the income tax rate. The purpose of this chapter is to examine the relationship among a variety of tax and benefit parameters in alternative schemes, and thereby to consider a wider range of trade-offs facing policy makers. The objective is not to undertake the enormous task of computing precise tax rates for a particular economy; rather, the chapter aims to provide a basic framework which is capable of providing some indication of the orders of magnitude involved in the trade-offs. The analysis therefore abstracts from many complications. Section 5.2 begins by presenting a general approach, based on the specification of the government's budget constraint. Section 5.3 adds more structural detail to the general model by considering specific tax schedules and means-testing arrangements. The section indicates how more complex tax structures could be accommodated by the general approach.

Two special cases are selected for further analysis. First, a means-tested flat-rate pension is financed from income tax revenue alone; this system is chosen to represent a stylised version of the age pension scheme in Australia. Secondly, a flat-rate universal pension is financed from several taxes, including income, payroll and consumption taxation. The second scheme corresponds to a stylised version of the flat-rate component of the UK pension scheme. Both cases obviously involve many simplifications; for details of the Australian and UK schemes, see Creedy and Disney (1989a,b) and Dilnot *et al.* (1994). Section 5.4 examines the means-tested scheme, while section 5.5 considers the trade-offs in the multi-tax universal pension scheme. Some technical details of the trade-offs are placed in an appendix.

5.1   A General Approach

Government pension and tax systems are usually very complex. In order to concentrate on the major issues involved, it is necessary to consider simplified systems which nevertheless capture the main elements of those used in practice. The analysis concentrates on the problem of financing a basic flat-rate pension, thereby ignoring earnings-related pensions. Problems associated with dependants' benefits are ignored and the models abstract from differences in household composition. In addition, eligibility conditions, which often depend on work histories, are ignored. Hence just two groups are considered: those over retirement age are all 'pensioners', and those below pension age are all workers. The aged dependency ratio is thus defined as the number of pensioners divided by the number of workers; it would be possible to add considerations such as labour-force participation and unemployment to the model, but these would be expected to change tax and benefit levels rather than the nature of trade-offs. Define the following terms:

b = Flat-rate pension received by all pensioners

N_w = Number of workers

N_p = Number of pensioners

Y = Total gross income of workers and pensioners combined

Y_T = Total taxable income of workers and pensioners combined

C = Payroll tax raised from earnings of workers

T_p = 'Pension tax' paid per pensioner (arising from means-testing)

E = Non-pension government expenditure per person

Suppose the income tax paid by each individual is a constant proportion, t, of *taxable* income, however defined. In addition there is a consumption tax in which all tax-exclusive expenditure is taxed at the fixed rate, v. Hence the equivalent rate expressed as a tax-inclusive rate applied to gross expenditure is $v/(1+v)$. There is also a payroll tax based on the gross earnings of workers. The existence of means-testing of the pension may be modelled in terms of what may be called a special 'pension tax' as described below.

The central element of the analysis is the budget constraint facing the government. This requires that total expenditure is equal to total revenue. Total expenditure is composed of non-pension expenditure, $E(N_w+N_p)$, plus the cost of the pension, $N_p b$. Total revenue is the sum of income taxation, tY_t, the pension tax, $N_p T_p$, the payroll tax, C, and the consumption tax. The latter is obtained by multiplying total disposable income, $Y - tY_t - N_p T_p - C$, by the tax-inclusive rate $v/(1 + v)$. Hence the constraint may be written as:

$$E\left(N_w + N_p\right) + N_p b = tY_T + N_p T_p + C + \frac{v}{1 + v}\left(Y - tY_T - N_p T_p - C\right) \quad (5.1)$$

In evaluating the total revenue from the consumption tax, the final term in (5.1), this formulation abstracts from individuals' savings. But it would be possible to modify (5.1) to allow for differing saving propensities of workers and pensioners. Equation (5.1) can be arranged as follows:

$$tY_T = (1 + v)\{E(N_w + N_p) + N_pb\} - vY - N_pT_p - C \qquad (5.2)$$

Further insight can be obtained by using the following relationships. If $\overline{w}$ and $\overline{y}$ denote the arithmetic mean income of workers and pensioners respectively, then:

$$Y = N_w\overline{w} + N_p\overline{y} \qquad (5.3)$$

Denote by γ the proportion of workers' aggregate gross income which is taxable. Suppose that, in order to avoid double taxation, the 'pension tax' paid by pensioners is deducted from their taxable income. In the system considered below, the total taxable income of pensioners is equal to their non-pension income less the 'pension tax' paid. Hence:

$$Y_T = \gamma N_w\overline{w} + N_p\left(\overline{y} - T_p\right) \qquad (5.4)$$

On the simplifying assumption that all worker's incomes are from employment, and that the payroll tax involves a proportional tax imposed at the rate c on a proportion, α, of gross earnings, then:

$$C = \alpha c N_w\overline{w} \qquad (5.5)$$

Similarly, the pension tax per pensioner arising from means-testing may be expressed as a proportion, β, of average pensioners' income, so that:

$$T_p = \beta\overline{y} \qquad (5.6)$$

Hence, if the replacement ratio, R, is defined as $b/\overline{y}$ and the aged dependency ratio, D, is N_p/N_w, equation (5.2) may be written as:

$$t = \frac{(1 + v)\{DR + (1 + D)(E/\overline{w})\} - v\left\{1 + D\left(\overline{y/\overline{w}}\right)\right\} - \beta D\left(\overline{y}/\overline{w}\right) - \alpha c}{\gamma + D\left(\overline{y}/\overline{w}\right)(1 - \beta)}$$
$$(5.7)$$

This result shows that the proportional tax rate is a function of a variety of components and is not as simple as is often suggested. The usual approach amounts to the assumption that $\alpha = \beta = v = \overline{y} = 0$ and $\gamma = 1$, so that (5.7) reduces simply to $t = DR + (1 + D)(E/\overline{w})$ and the relevant trade-offs are immediately obvious. Very few policy choices are available in this simple format. In (5.7) the dependency ratio, D, enters in a much more complex manner. In order to make further progress it is thus necessary to specify the tax structure in more detail.

The general result in (5.7) can be used to examine the implications of a wide variety of schemes. However, care must be taken in modifying (5.7) when there is no means-testing but pensioners' incomes are otherwise taken into account. Without means testing, $\beta = 0$, but it is usual to have a tax-free threshold applied to pensioners incomes. This makes the taxable income of pensioners some proportion, δ, of pensioners' gross income. Hence (5.4) must be replaced by:

$$Y_T = \gamma N_w \overline{w} + \delta N_p \overline{y} \qquad (5.8)$$

and the denominator of (5.7) becomes $\gamma + \delta D (\overline{y}/\overline{w})$. The following section presents in further detail the various components of the tax structure which are included in (5.7).

5.2 Specification of Tax Structures

The general form of the budget constraint in (5.7) involves various proportions which depend on the precise form of the tax structure. These include the proportion of workers' incomes which is taxable, γ, the proportion of workers' incomes subject to the payroll tax, α, the proportion of pensioners' income which is taxable, δ, and the 'pension tax' rate imposed on the retired, β, resulting from means-testing. This section derives the proportions for particular tax structures.

5.2.1 Income tax

Suppose there is a single marginal tax rate applied to all income measured above a tax-free threshold. If a worker's income is denoted by w, and the tax-free threshold applied to workers is a, the income tax paid, $T(w)$, is given by:

$$
\begin{aligned}
T(w) &= 0 \qquad \text{for } w \le a \\
&= t(w - a) \text{ for } w > a
\end{aligned}
\tag{5.9}
$$

Let $F(w)$ denote the distribution function of wage income. Using the income tax system in (5.9) it can be shown that the proportion of total workers' income which is taxed, γ, is given by:

$$
\gamma = \{1 - F_1(a)\} - \left(\frac{a}{\overline{w}}\right)\{1 - F(a)\}
\tag{5.10}
$$

where $F_1(a)$ denotes the proportion of total income of those workers with $w \le a$, so that F_1 is the 'incomplete first moment' distribution function of F. Hence if $a = 0$, then $F_1(0) = F(0) = 0$ and $\gamma = 1$. Equation (5.10) is obtained by simplifying $\gamma = \int_a^\infty (w - a)\, dF(w)/\overline{w}$. This simple structure is a good approximation to the UK income tax but in Australia there is more progression in the rate structure. Equation (5.10) can, however, be expanded to deal with a multiple rate structure, by appropriate summation. In order to concentrate on the nature of pension trade-offs, the following presentation retains the use of a single marginal rate (which may in fact be interpreted as an appropriately weighted average of several rates).

If there is no means-testing of the pension, and if the tax threshold for pensioners is the same as for workers, the tax function facing pensioners, $T_r(y)$, is, assuming that the pension is included in taxable income:

$$
\begin{aligned}
T_r(y) &= 0 \qquad\qquad \text{for } y + b \le a \\
&= \{t(y + b) - a\} \text{ for } y + b > a
\end{aligned}
\tag{5.11}
$$

When $b > a$, all pensioners pay income taxation, so that δ, the ratio of taxable income to gross income, is $1 + (b - a)/\overline{y}$. But if $b < a$, all those with incomes below $a - b$ will not pay tax and if $H(y)$ denotes the distribution function of y, the value of δ is given by:

$$\delta = \{1 - H_1 (a - b)\} - \{(a - b) / \overline{y}\} \{1 - H (a - b)\} \tag{5.12}$$

where $H_1(a - b)$ denotes the proportion of total income of those pensioners with $y < a - b$, so that H_1 is the incomplete first moment distribution function of H. Equations (5.10) and (5.12) obviously take the same basic form. In practice, the taxation of the income of pensioners is complicated by regulations concerning the taxation of annuity income (and the source of funds used to purchase annuities), but these complications are ignored here.

5.2.2 A Means-tested Pension

Suppose pensioners receive a pension which is means-tested according to gross income. If income is below a lower limit, y_e, then the full pension is received. When y exceeds y_e, the pension is reduced by a proportion, s, of income in excess of the lower limit. Thus the pension is reduced by an amount $s(y - y_e)$. This implies that no pension is received once y reaches an upper limit, y_u, which is equal to $y_e + b/s$. This income test is very similar to that used in Australia. There is also an asset test in Australia, but the income test is the one that is relevant to the vast majority of the retired, so the asset test is ignored here.

An equivalent way of viewing this type of income test is to regard each retired individual as receiving an unconditional pension of b, but also paying a special 'pension tax' on non-pension income. The regulations stated in the previous paragraph can be converted into a pension tax schedule, $P(y)$, given by:

$$
\begin{aligned}
P(y) &= 0 && \text{for } y \leq y_e & (5.13) \\
&= s(y - y_e) && \text{for } y_e < y < y_u & \\
&= b && \text{for } y \geq y_u & (5.14)
\end{aligned}
$$

Hence those above y_u pay a 'pension tax' that is exactly the same as the pension received. In assessing each pensioner for income taxation, it is necessary to avoid double taxation of the pension tax by making it tax-deductible.

Suppose the income tax threshold for pensioners is a_r. Then the income tax paid, $T_r(y)$, is given by:

$$T_r(y) = t\left[(y+b) - \{a_r + P(y)\}\right] \tag{5.15}$$

Here $y + b$ is total income and $a_r + P(y)$ measures the effective total allowance against that income for tax purposes. The following analysis uses the assumption, following the Australian system, that $b = a_r$, so that $T_r(y)$ can be rewritten simply as:

$$T_r(y) = t\{y - P(y)\} \tag{5.16}$$

Thus taxable income is equal to non-pension income less the amount of pension tax paid. It can be shown that the ratio, β, of pension tax per pensioner to average income, $\bar{y}$, is:

$$\beta = \left(\frac{b}{\bar{y}}\right)\{1 - H(y_u)\} + s\{H_1(y_u) - H_1(y_e)\} - s\left(\frac{y_e}{\bar{y}}\right)\{H(y_u) - H(y_e)\} \tag{5.17}$$

where $H_1(y)$ represents, as before, the proportion of total income obtained by those pensioners with incomes less than or equal to y. The first term in curly brackets in (5.17) represents the proportion of pensioners who pay the maximum pension tax of b; the second term in curly brackets represents the total income of those who pay pension tax at the rate, s; the third term in curly brackets denotes the proportion of pensioners who pay the pension tax.

5.2.3   The Payroll Tax

The payroll tax $C(w)$, is assumed to be a constant proportion, c, of the gross income of workers, applied between two limits w_e and w_u. The UK system of National Insurance Contributions took this form for some years (ignoring employers' contributions), and more formally it is given by:

$$C(w) \;\; = \;\; 0 \qquad \text{for } w < w_e \tag{5.18}$$

$$= cw \quad \text{for } w_e \leq w < w_u$$

$$= cw_u \quad \text{for } w \geq w_u \tag{5.19}$$

It can be shown that the proportion, α, of workers' total income that is taxable is given by:

$$\alpha = \{F_1(w_u) - F_1(w_e)\} + \left(\frac{w_u}{\overline{w}}\right)\{1 - F(w_u)\} \tag{5.20}$$

The first term reflects the proportion of total income of those with income between the limits w_e and w_u, while the second term reflects the fact that all those above the upper limit w_u pay a fixed contribution. Equation (5.20) is obtained by simplifying the expression:

$$\alpha = \left\{\int_{w_e}^{w_u} w \, dF(w) + w_u \int_{w_u}^{\infty} dF(w)\right\} / \overline{w} \tag{5.21}$$

The framework set out in section 5.2 can be used to consider a wide range of pension and tax structures. This chapter concentrates on just two structures for comparison purposes. In the first scheme a means-tested pension is combined with only an income tax, as a simplified version of the system in Australia. Appropriate substitution into (5.7) gives the budget constraint as:

$$t = \frac{DR + (1+D)(E/\overline{w}) - \beta D(\overline{y}/\overline{w})}{\gamma + D(\overline{y}/\overline{w})(1-\beta)} \tag{5.22}$$

In the second scheme, a pension is combined with the payroll, income and consumption taxes, but there is no means-testing. This is similar to the UK scheme. Appropriate substitution gives:

$$t = \frac{(1+v)\{DR + (1+D)(E/\overline{w})\} - v\{1 + D(\overline{y}/\overline{w})\} - \alpha c}{\gamma + \delta D(\overline{y}/\overline{w})} \tag{5.23}$$

The two results in (5.22) and (5.23) are used in sections 5.4 and 5.5 below, which examine the trade-offs involved in a number of policy choices.

5.3   Trade-offs in the Means-tested System

The result in equation (5.22) can be used to examine the implications for selected tax parameters of changes in any parameter of the pension system, if it is required to keep non-pension expenditure fixed. Changes in the basic pension, b, or the pension tax rate, s, which are accompanied by changes in the basic rate of income tax are not revenue neutral since they imply different levels of gross government expenditure, but they are deficit neutral in the sense that E is unchanged. The examination of such trade-offs is not straightforward because of the complexity of the budget constraint.

5.3.1   Changes in b and t

Consider first a change in the pension which is financed by an increase in the marginal rate of income tax. For deficit neutrality, the combination of changes in these two parameters must satisfy:

$$\frac{dt}{db} = -\frac{\partial E/\partial b}{\partial E/\partial t} \tag{5.24}$$

Rearrangement of (5.22) and differentiation with respect to t gives:

$$\frac{\partial E}{\partial t} = \frac{\gamma \overline{w} + (1 - \beta) D \overline{y}}{D + 1} \tag{5.25}$$

which is positive since g and b are between zero and one. Similarly:

$$\frac{\partial E}{\partial b} = \frac{D}{D + 1} \left[\overline{y} (1 - t) \frac{\partial \beta}{\partial b} - 1 \right] \tag{5.26}$$

Partial differentiation of (5.17) with respect to b gives:

$$\frac{\partial \beta}{\partial b} = (1/\overline{y}) [1 - H(y_u)] \tag{5.27}$$

which is positive and a function of b, since y_u depends on b. Substituting (5.27) in (5.26) produces:

$$\frac{\partial E}{\partial b} = \frac{D}{D + 1} [(1 - t) \{1 - H(y_u)\} - 1] \tag{5.28}$$

which is negative since $(1 - t)$ and $\{1 - H(y_u)\}$ are positive. Substituting (5.25) and (5.28) in (5.24) gives:

$$\frac{dt}{db} = \frac{D\left[1 - (1 - t)\{1 - H(y_u)\}\right]}{\gamma\overline{w} + (1 - \beta)D\overline{y}} \tag{5.29}$$

which is positive and a function of t and b. This means that for given values of the other variables, an increase in the basic pension requires an increase in the income tax rate, the magnitude of which depends on the initial levels of t and b.

The numerical evaluation of (5.29) involves the terms γ and β, given in (5.10) and (5.17) respectively, along with the averages $\overline{w}$ and $\overline{y}$ and the integral $H(y_u)$. In the calculations reported below, the assumption is made that w and y can be described by the lognormal distribution. This allows the various integrals to be evaluated using a poynomial approximation given in Aitchison and Brown (1957). Any functional form must of course be regarded as an approximation to the actual distribution of income, but the lognormal has a very long history in income distribution studies of providing a good description of the complete range of incomes (although the fit is typically less good in the upper tail).

The following examples were obtained using the assumption that w and y are lognormally distributed with variance of logarithms of 0.3 and 0.5. The mean of logarithms of w and y are chosen so that the arithmetic mean, $\overline{w}$, is equal to \$40,000 and $\overline{y}$ is \$16,000. The purpose of the exercise is to provide some indication of the orders of magnitude involved in the trade-offs, which are by no means obvious from the formulae. The values used to 'calibrate' the model are chosen as being representative only, although much care has been taken in selecting values which are appropriate for the present contexts of Australia and the UK. Fully documented computer programs are available for those wishing to examine alternative assumptions.

For a 'pension tax' rate of 0.5, a pension of \$8,000, and dependency ratio of 0.2, the required marginal income tax rate is 0.262 and it is found that $1000(dt/db)$ is 0.00527. If the pension is \$4,000 the income tax rate is 0.242 and $1000(dt/db)$ is 0.00448. A higher pension of \$12,000 requires an income tax rate of 0.284 and a value of $1000(dt/db)$ of 0.00547. For larger values of b, the values of dt/db are constant. For a higher 'pension tax' rate, higher pensions are required before the relationship between t and b becomes linear. The major result is thus that an increase in the pension of $1,000 requires approximately half a percentage point added to the tax rate.

5.3.2   Changes in s and t

Consider next the policy option of changing the 'pension tax' rate, s, financed by a change in the income tax rate such that E remains constant. For changes in s and t, this requires:

$$\frac{dt}{ds} = -\frac{\partial E/\partial s}{\partial E/\partial t} \tag{5.30}$$

Appropriate differentiation gives:

$$\frac{\partial E}{\partial s} = \frac{D\bar{y}\,(1-t)}{D+1}\frac{\partial \beta}{\partial s} \tag{5.31}$$

Substituting (5.25) and (5.31) in (5.30) gives:

$$\frac{dt}{ds} = -\left[\frac{D\bar{y}\,(1-t)}{g_\gamma \bar{w} + (1-\beta)\,D\bar{y}}\right]\frac{\partial \beta}{\partial s} \tag{5.32}$$

where:

$$\frac{\partial \beta}{\partial s} = [H_1\,(y_u) - H_1\,(y_e)] - \left(\frac{y_e}{\bar{y}}\right)[H\,(y_u) - H\,(y_e)] \tag{5.33}$$

If K represents the term in square brackets in (5.32), then since t, γ and β are positive and ≤ 1, K is positive. The sign of dt/ds therefore depends on the sign of $\partial \beta/\partial s$. From (5.33), $\partial \beta/\partial s$ is positive if:

$$\frac{H_1\,(y_u) - H_1\,(y_e)}{H\,(y_u) - H\,(y_e)} > \frac{y_e}{\bar{y}} \tag{5.34}$$

For practical purposes, $y_e/\bar{y}$ is less than 1. For example, for $y_e = \$2,000$ and $\bar{y} = \$8,000$, $\partial \beta/\partial s$ is positive if the term on the left-hand side of (5.41) is greater than 0.25. Calculations indicate that this condition is satisfied for virtually any pension taper rate, regardless of the magnitude of the basic pension and the dependency ratio. Further insight into (5.42) can be obtained by recognising that the left-hand side represents the slope of a straight line joining two points on a Lorenz curve (which plots the relationship between H_1 and H). Thus, so long as y is not too unequally distributed, an increase in the 'pension tax' rate is associated with a decrease in the marginal income tax rate. The magnitude of dt/ds is not constant but depends on the initial income and pension tax rates.

5.3.3 Changing y_e and t

The policy option of changing the 'pension tax threshold', y_e, financed by a change in the income tax rate such that E remains constant is analysed using:

$$\frac{dt}{dy_e} = -\frac{\partial E / \partial y_e}{\partial E / \partial t} \qquad (5.35)$$

Appropriate differentiation gives:

$$\frac{\partial E}{\partial y_e} = \frac{D\bar{y}\,(1-t)}{D+1}\frac{\partial \beta}{\partial y_e} \qquad (5.36)$$

with:

$$\frac{\partial \beta}{\partial y_e} = -\,(s/\bar{y})\,[H\,(y_u) - H\,(y_e)] \qquad (5.37)$$

which is negative. Substitution of (5.36) and (5.37) in (5.35) gives:

$$\frac{dt}{dy_e} = -K\frac{\partial \beta}{\partial y_e} \qquad (5.38)$$

which is positive and not constant. Note that K in (5.38) is evaluated for different values of y_e, whereas K in (5.32) is evaluated for different values of s. Not unexpectedly, an increase in the pension tax threshold is associated with an increase in the income tax rate.

For example, for a 'pension tax' rate of 0.5, dependency ratio of 0.2, basic pension of $8,000 and pension tax threshold of $2,000, the required income tax rate is 0.262; it is found that $1000(dt/dy_e) = 0.00180$. If the pension tax threshold is much higher, at $10,000, the required income tax rate increases to 0.27, but $1000(dt/dy_e)$ decreases to 0.00046. Because $y_u = b/s + y_e$, for a given basic pension, an increase in s can be offset by an increase in y_e. For example, an income tax rate of 0.262 is also required for the higher taper rate of 0.8 and the higher pension tax threshold of $4,000.

One policy choice that is not 'marginal', and hence is not represented by the types of formulae given here, was proposed by Gruen (1985, p.621). He suggested that the taper rate or pension tax rate in Australia should be reduced 'to 25 per cent or at most 33 per cent' and that this could be financed by setting $y_e = 0$. Further calculations based on (5.22) show that Gruen's 'educated guess' concerning the trade-off was reasonably good, although an increase in the tax rate (of less than one percentage point) would also be needed for deficit neutrality.

5.4 Trade-offs in the Multi-tax System

With the multi-tax system corresponding to that in the UK, the government's constraint in (5.23) can be used to analyse changes in components of the structure. Further details are again given in the appendix.

5.4.1 Changes in b and t

Consider changing the basic pension and the income tax rate while E remains unchanged. Differentiation of E with respect to t,using (5.23), gives:

$$\frac{\partial E}{\partial t} = \frac{\gamma \overline{w} + \delta D \overline{y}}{(1+v)(D+1)} \tag{5.39}$$

Similarly:

$$\frac{\partial E}{\partial b} = \frac{1}{(1+v)(D+1)} \left[t D \overline{y} \frac{\partial \delta}{\partial b} - D \right] \tag{5.40}$$

Substitution of (5.39) and (5.40) results in:

$$\frac{dt}{db} = \frac{-D \left[t \overline{y} \frac{\partial \delta}{\partial b} - 1 \right]}{\gamma \overline{w} + \delta D \overline{y}} \tag{5.41}$$

Two cases need to be distinguished in obtaining an expression for $\partial\delta/\partial b$. Consider first the case when $b \geq a$, for which, as shown above, $\delta = 1 + (b - a)/\overline{y}$ and:

$$\frac{\partial\delta}{\partial b} = \frac{1}{\overline{y}} \tag{5.42}$$

which can be substituted into (5.41). The proportion δ is positive and a function of b. Consequently, dt/db is positive but not constant, being a function of both t and b. Secondly, the case of $b < a$ is obtained by partial differentiation of (5.12) which gives:

$$\frac{\partial\delta}{\partial b} = \left[\{\overline{y} + a - b\} h(a - b) + \{1 - H(a - b)\}\right]/\overline{y} \tag{5.43}$$

where $h(.)$ is the density associated with $H(.)$. In this case $\partial\delta/\partial b$ is also positive but the sign of dt/db depends on the magnitude of the term $t\overline{y}(\partial\delta/\partial b)$. With a mean pensioner income of \$8,000, for practical purposes dt/db is positive for $b < a$ as well as for $b \geq a$. For example, for an income tax threshold of \$5,000, a dependency ratio of 0.2 and $v = c = 0$, the income tax rate corresponding to a pension of \$2,000 is 0.244 and $1000(dt/db)$ is 0.00304. This income tax rate is comparable with that in the means-tested system. However, with $v = 0.15$ and $c = 0.075$, the required income tax rate is much lower, at 0.027; in this case $1000(dt/db)$ is 0.00528. A higher pension of \$4,000 implies an income tax rate of 0.037 and a similar $1000(dt/db)$ of 0.00529.

5.4.2 Changes in v and t

The deficit neutral relationship between the income tax rate and the consumption tax rate requires:

$$\frac{dt}{dv} = -\frac{\partial E/\partial v}{\partial E/\partial t} \tag{5.44}$$

Using:

$$\frac{\partial E}{\partial v} = \frac{(1 - t\gamma - c\alpha)\overline{w} + D\overline{y}(1 - t\delta) + Db}{(D + 1)(1 + v^2)} \tag{5.45}$$

Substitution of (5.25) and (5.45) in (5.47) gives:

$$\frac{dt}{dv} = \frac{-\{(1 - t\gamma - c\alpha)\,\overline{w} + D\overline{y}\,(1 - t\delta) + Db\}}{(1 + v)\,(\gamma\overline{w} + \delta D\overline{y})} \tag{5.46}$$

Since t, γ, $c\alpha$ and δ are positive fractions, dt/dv is negative and not constant. This means that an increase in the consumption tax rate is, as might be expected, associated with a decrease in the income tax rate. For practical purposes, it appears that dt/dv is constant for a given basic pension. With $v = c = 0$, a dependency ratio of 0.2 and a basic pension of \$8,000, the income tax rate is 0.269 and dt/dv is -0.89247. If $v = 0.10$, the income tax rate is 0.18 and dt/dv is unchanged at -0.89247. Furthermore, if $c = 0.085$, the income tax rate is 0.103 but dt/dv is unchanged. If the pension is \$10,000 the tax rate is 0.112 and dt/dv is -0.88298.

5.4.3   Changes in c and t

Finally, the deficit neutral relationship between the income tax rate and the payroll tax rate is obtained from:

$$\frac{dt}{dc} = -\frac{\partial E/\partial c}{\partial E/\partial t} \tag{5.47}$$

Using:

$$\frac{\partial E}{\partial c} = \frac{\alpha\overline{w}}{(1 + v)\,(D + 1)} \tag{5.48}$$

Appropriate substituting in (5.47) gives:

$$\frac{dt}{dc} = -\frac{\overline{w}\alpha}{\gamma\overline{w} + \delta D\overline{y}} \tag{5.49}$$

which is negative and constant. For example, for a $v = 0.15$ and $c = 0.075$, a dependency ratio of 0.2 and a pension of \$8,000, the required tax rate is 0.058 and $dt/dc = -1.02515$. As in the case of v, dt/dc only changes for different values of the basic pension. Thus an increase in c is associated with a constant proportional decrease in the income tax rate.

5.5 Conclusions

The aim of this chapter has been to examine the nature of policy trade-offs involved in different pension and tax structures. After presenting a general analysis of the government's budget constraint, the chapter concentrated on two basic types of scheme. The first, using a means-tested pension and only income taxation, is similar to the Australian scheme; the second is closer to the flat-rate component of the UK pension scheme, and has consumption and payroll taxes in addition to income taxation, but no means-testing.

For representative parameter values, it was found that an increase in the pension of \$1,000 in the means-tested scheme requires an increase in the income tax rate of just under one-half of one percentage point. When there is no means-testing, the required increase in the income tax rate is just over one-half of one percentage point. In the means-tested system, an increase in the threshold income level above which the 'pension tax' applies, by \$1,000, requires an increase in the income tax rate of just under one-fifth of one percentage point.

In the multi-tax (no means-testing) scheme, an increase in the consumption tax rate of one percentage point is associated with a decrease in the income tax rate of about nine-tenths of a percentage point. The difference partly reflects the fact that the tax base for consumption is slightly lower than for income taxation. However, an increase in the payroll tax rate of one percentage point is associated with a decrease in the income tax rate of about one and two-tenths percentage points. Despite the upper limit on the payroll tax, this is applied to gross income, unlike the income tax which has a tax-free threshold. Debates concerning population ageing have typically focused on a very simple model in which there is an obvious relationship between pension levels, the aged dependency ratio and the income tax rate. The chapter has shown that the range of policy choices available to governments is substantially greater, given the number of relevant policy variables. Furthermore, the nature of the government's budget constraint is rather complex, so that the trade-offs are not immediately obvious. Hence illustrative orders of magnitude have been reported.

Chapter 6

Private versus Public Pensions

The condition under which a compulsory pay-as-you-go pension system, in which the current generation of workers finances the pensions of the current retired generation, is superior to the use of private saving in order to finance a future retirement income, has been well-known since the work of Samuelson (1958) and Aaron (1966); for a review of the issues and literature, see Disney (1996). Using a simple two-period overlapping generations model, they showed that a transfer system is superior if (approximately) the sum of the rates of growth of population and real earnings exceed the real rate of interest. Section 6.1 below presents the basic two-period model for the case where earnings are fixed.

The present chapter extends the results to the case where some individuals in each cohort live longer, in a three-period model, but where different generations of retired persons alive at the same time are given a different pension. This issue is examined in section 6.2. A major purpose of the chapter is to extend the two-period model to allow for labour supply responses to taxation. Hence the attempt to raise revenue in order to finance current pensions introduces distortions into labour supply and a reduction in the tax base. This is the subject of section 6.3. The optimal tax rate is derived and the conditions under which the Samuelson-Aaron condition is unchanged are examined; this essentially applies to combinations of productivity and population growth and real interest rates for which the optimal tax rate is zero. Productivity growth rates required in order to support alternative optimal tax rates are also examined.

6.1 A Two-period Model

Suppose that individuals live for two periods. In the first period, each individual receives the income of y, while in the second, a period of retirement, income is zero. Consumption in each period is denoted c_1 and c_2 respectively. All variables are in real terms. Write the lifetime utility of each individual, U, as the additively separable form:

$$U = c_1^\beta + \frac{1}{1+\xi}c_2^\beta \tag{6.1}$$

where ξ denotes the rate of time preference and $\eta = 1/(1-\beta)$ is the intertemporal elasticity of substitution between consumption in the two periods.

6.1.1 Private Pensions

With no tax and transfer system, utility is maximised subject to the lifetime budget constraint:

$$y = c_1 + \frac{1}{1+r}c_2 \tag{6.2}$$

where r is the fixed real rate of interest at which individuals can borrow and lend. Borrowing constraints are ignored (since in the present context only lending is relevant). The Lagrangean is:

$$L = c_1^\beta + \frac{1}{1+\xi}c_2^\beta + \lambda \left[y - c_1 - \frac{1}{1+r}c_2 \right] \tag{6.3}$$

The first-order conditions, in addition to the budget constraint, are $\frac{\partial L}{\partial c_1} = \beta c_1^{\beta-1} - \lambda = 0$ and $\frac{\partial L}{\partial c_2} = \frac{\beta}{1+\xi}c_2^{\beta-1} - \frac{\lambda}{1+r} = 0$. It can be shown that the solution to this problem is:

$$c_1 = y\theta \tag{6.4}$$

$$c_2 = yk\theta \tag{6.5}$$

where k and θ are:

$$k = \left(\frac{1+r}{1+\xi}\right)^{\eta} \tag{6.6}$$

$$\theta = \left(1 + \frac{k}{1+r}\right)^{-1} \tag{6.7}$$

The savings rate in the first period is thus $1 - \theta$ and accumulated savings in the second period are therefore equal to $y(1 - \theta)(1 + r)$. It can be shown that $(1 - \theta)(1 + r) = k\theta$, which establishes that savings can indeed finance the planned consumption of $yk\theta$.

6.1.2 Social Transfers

Suppose that, instead of financing consumption in the second period using private savings, a proportional tax is imposed on the working population at the same rate as the saving rate that would otherwise arise. Hence the current retired generation is supported by the next generation of workers. If income grows at the rate δ, then the tax base per person is increased to $(1 + \delta) y$. If the size of the current working population is the same as that of the current population of the retired, and the pension per person is p, then from the governments budget constraint:

$$p = y(1+\delta)(1-\theta) \tag{6.8}$$

It has been mentioned above that $(1 - \theta)(1 + r) = k\theta$, so that substituting for $(1 - \theta)$ in(6.8) gives:

$$p = yk\theta\left(\frac{1+\delta}{1+r}\right) \tag{6.9}$$

Hence the pension exceeds the consumption that would otherwise be available from private savings if $p > c_2$, with c_2 given from equation (6.5). This requires:

$$\delta > r \tag{6.10}$$

and the growth rate of real income must exceed the real rate of interest. The transfer payment, or pension, provides a constant ratio of current pension to current income.

If the population grows at a rate of ρ, there is one pensioner for every $(1 + \rho)$ workers. The application of the same tax rate gives a new pension of:

$$p = yk\theta \frac{(1 + \rho)(1 + \delta)}{(1 + r)} \tag{6.11}$$

and the transfer payment exceeds the consumption from private savings if:

$$\delta + \rho + \rho\delta > r \tag{6.12}$$

It is often assumed that $\rho\delta \cong 0$, in which case the sum of the population and productivity growth rates must exceed the real rate of interest. However, in this type of two-period model the values of δ and ρ are much larger than in an annual context, so it is appropriate to retain the product term. If the population is ageing and ρ is negative, the transfer system can make each generation better off so long as:

$$|\rho| < \frac{\delta - r}{1 + \delta} \tag{6.13}$$

6.2 Higher Longevity

Suppose that people expect to live longer than the two periods considered above. If the probability of living for another period in retirement is s, each individual's problem, in the absence of social transfers, is to maximise:

$$U = c_1^\beta + \frac{1}{1 + \xi} c_2^\beta + \frac{s}{(1 + \xi)^2} c_3^\beta \tag{6.14}$$

6.2.1 Private Pensions

In the absence of a tax and transfer system, the constraint facing each individual is:

$$y = c_1 + \frac{1}{1+r}c_2 + \frac{1}{(1+r)^2}c_3 \qquad (6.15)$$

Following the above procedure, this can be solved to give consumption in each period as:

$$c_1 = y\theta' \qquad (6.16)$$

$$c_2 = yk\theta' \qquad (6.17)$$

$$c_3 = syk^2\theta' \qquad (6.18)$$

where:

$$\theta' = \left[1 + \frac{k}{1+r} + s\left(\frac{k}{1+r}\right)^2\right]^{-1} \qquad (6.19)$$

and k is the same as in (6.6). The saving rate during the working period is $1 - \theta'$.

It might be argued that if the probability of surviving for the third period is s, there is a probability, equal to $1-s$, of each member of the current generation of workers receiving an inheritance equal to the planned consumption for the third period of those who were workers two periods previously. The value of the inheritance is, from (6.18), therefore $sy_{-2}k^2\theta'$, where $y_{-2} = y/\left(1+\delta\right)^2$. The above results can be modified by substituting y' for y, where y' is the expected value of the sum of income and the inheritance, given by:

$$y' = y\left[1 + \frac{s\left(1-s\right)k^2\theta'}{\left(1+\delta\right)^2}\right] \qquad (6.20)$$

6.2.2   Social Transfers

In the case where private savings are replaced by an inter-generational transfer system, consider the application of the saving rate, $1-\theta'$, as a proportional tax rate imposed on the current generation of workers. This raises a revenue, supposing that the inheritance is also taxable, of $\left(1 - \theta'\right)y'$. For each worker there are $1/(1+\rho)$ people in the first period of retirement and $s/(1+\rho)^2$ in the second period of retirement.

Suppose that the tax revenue is used to pay pensions. It is possible to distinguish retirees according to their cohort, so assume that different pensions are paid to each generation at the same date. Let p and πp denote the pensions paid to those currently in their first and second period of retirement respectively. One method of determining the value of π would be to take the ratio of planned consumption in the two periods under the private scheme, so that from (6.16) and (6.17), $\pi = sk$.

The government's budget constraint for the transfer system is:

$$(1-\theta')\,y' = \frac{p}{1+\rho} + \frac{s\pi p}{(1+\rho)^2} \tag{6.21}$$

and p is given by:

$$p = y'\,(1-\theta')\,(1+\rho)\left\{1+\frac{s\pi}{1+\rho}\right\}^{-1} \tag{6.22}$$

The question then arises of how the pension compares with the consumption that would otherwise be provided under a private scheme. From equation (6.16), it can be seen that the private consumption that would otherwise be provided by the cohort currently in its first period of retirement is equal to $y'k\theta'/(1+\delta)$. Hence that cohort is better off if:

$$p > \frac{y'k\theta'}{1+\delta} \tag{6.23}$$

Those currently in their second period of retirement are better off than they would be under private provision if:

$$\pi p = \frac{sy'k^2\theta'}{(1+\delta)^2} \tag{6.24}$$

and as $\pi = sk$, this condition reduces to a comparison involving the replacement rate during the first period of retirement, so that only condition (6.23) needs to be applied. Hence social transfers can improve the welfare of each generation, compared with private saving, if:

$$\delta > \frac{k\theta' \left(1 + \rho + s^2 k\right)}{\left(1 - \theta'\right)\left(1 + \rho\right)^2} - 1 \tag{6.25}$$

It can be confirmed that if $s = 0$, condition (6.25) reduces to the requirement that $(1 + \delta)(1 + \rho) > (1 + r)$, which is exactly the same as in the two-period model. The simplification of (6.25) uses the convenient result that $(1 - \theta)(1 + r) = k\theta$, noted in section 6.1.

6.3 Labour Supply Variations

The two-period model examined in section 6.1 assumes that the income of each person in the working period is exogenously fixed. The imposition of the tax and transfer system has no incentive effects. This section extends the model to allow for labour supply variations. The attempt to raise revenue to finance the inter-generational transfers therefore leads to a reduction in the tax base.

If the consumption of leisure in the first period is h, where this is measured as a proportion of the total time available that is spent in leisure, and if the utility function is Cobb-Douglas, then the modification of (6.1) gives, in logarithmic form:

$$U = \alpha \log c_1 + (1 - \alpha) \log h + \frac{\alpha}{1 + \xi} \log c_2 \tag{6.26}$$

6.3.1 Private Pensions

In the case where consumption in retirement is financed by private savings, U is maximised subject to the constraint:

$$c_1 + \frac{1}{1 + r} c_2 = w (1 - h) \tag{6.27}$$

where w is the fixed wage rate. Using the standard Cobb-Douglas results, the solution to this problem is:

$$c_1 = \frac{\alpha (1 + \xi)}{(1 + \alpha + \xi)} w \tag{6.28}$$

$$c_2 = \frac{\alpha\left(1+r\right)}{\left(1+\alpha+\xi\right)}w \qquad (6.29)$$

$$h = \frac{\left(1-\alpha\right)\left(1+\xi\right)}{\left(1+\alpha+\xi\right)} \qquad (6.30)$$

From (6.30), labour supply remains fixed irrespective of the wage rate, so that income and consumption grow at the same rate as the wage rate. This property of the Cobb-Douglas utility function applies only when there is no non-wage income, and therefore disappears when social transfers are introduced.

6.3.2   Social Transfers

The results of the previous subsection can be said to describe the private plans, in the absence of transfer payments, made during the first period of life of a generation or cohort denoted by the letter A. Consider next the case where there is a social transfer of p_A paid to that generation. This pension is financed by a proportional tax at the rate, t, imposed on the following generation, denoted by the letter B, during the period when they are workers. It is therefore necessary to consider the labour supply behaviour of generation B. As before, assume that there is productivity growth, implying that the wage rate faced by each member of generation B is $w\left(1+\delta\right)$; hence δ is applied to the wage rate rather than earnings. Following the standard approach, define the 'full income', M_B, of each worker in cohort B as:

$$M_B = \frac{p_B}{1+r} + w\left(1+\delta\right)\left(1-t\right) \qquad (6.31)$$

where p_B is the pension which each member of generation B expects to receive during retirement. In general, M varies between generations, and the solution to the optimisation problem for each generation is given by equations of the form:

$$c_1 = \frac{\alpha\left(1+\xi\right)}{\left(1+\alpha+\xi\right)}M \qquad (6.32)$$

$$c_2 = \frac{\alpha (1+r)}{(1+\alpha+\xi)} M \tag{6.33}$$

$$h = \frac{(1-\alpha)(1+\xi)}{(1+\alpha+\xi)} \frac{M}{w'(1-t)} \tag{6.34}$$

where w' is the appropriate wage for the generation being considered, which also enters into M.

Each worker in generation B, for which $w' = w(1+\delta)$, therefore obtains earnings of y_B, equal to $w(1+\delta)(1-h)$. Assuming that the wage rate exceeds the minimum wage necessary to generate an interior solution, appropriate substitution gives:

$$y_B = (1-\eta)(1+\delta)w - \frac{\eta}{1-t}\left(\frac{p_B}{1+r}\right) \tag{6.35}$$

where:

$$\eta = \frac{(1-\alpha)(1+\xi)}{1+\alpha+\xi} \tag{6.36}$$

With population growth at the rate, ρ, as before, the tax revenue available to finance the pension of each member of generation A is $t(1+\rho)y_B$, so the budget constraint facing the transfer system is:

$$p_A = t(1+\rho)y_B \tag{6.37}$$

A similar condition must also apply to the finance of generation B's pension, provided by a subsequent generation, say C, such that $p_B = t(1+\rho)y_C$, where y_C is obtained from a suitable modification of equation (6.35). It can be shown that if the pension is adjusted in line with the growth of the wage rate, such that $p_B = p_A(1+\delta)$, a constant tax rate, t, can be applied to each generation of workers. This means that the ratio of the pension to the current wage rate is constant over time; in the exogenous income case of section 6.1, the ratio of the pension to income is constant.

Applying this indexation rule, substitution of $p_B = p_A(1+\delta)$ into (6.35) and then substituting the result into (6.37) gives, after a little manipulation, the value of the tax rate required to satisfy the budget constraint as the solution to:

$$At^2 + \{(B - C)\,p_A - A\}\,t + Cp_A = 0 \tag{6.38}$$

where:

$$A = \alpha w \,(1 + \delta)\,(2 + \xi) \tag{6.39}$$

$$B = \frac{(1 + \delta)\,(1 - \alpha)\,(1 + \xi)}{(1 + r)} \tag{6.40}$$

$$C = \frac{(1 + \alpha + \xi)}{(1 + \rho)} \tag{6.41}$$

It is therefore possible to solve for the tax rate, t, required to finance a given pension, p_A, by taking the lowest positive root of (6.38) in the range $0 \le t < 1$. Depending on the parameter values, there may of course be only one feasible root in the range, or no real roots. Having solved for t, it is then possible to obtain the labour supply, consumption and hence utility of each member of generation B, using (6.32) to (6.34).

The above model allows for private savings, in addition to the pension, to be made if desired. For any set of parameters it is possible to find the value of t, and the associated pension, which maximises the utility of each member of generation B. The resulting value generates the optimal mixture of private and social provision of retirement incomes.

6.3.3 The Optimal Tax Rate

The first step in examining the optimal tax rate is to obtain the indirect utility function, expressing utility in terms of the pension, p, the tax rate, t, along with the wage rate, w. Consider cohort B, where substitution for c_1, c_2, h, and M_B into U gives, after some manipulation and using the monotonic transformation of the utility function such that $U = c_1^\alpha h^{(1-\alpha)} c_2^{\left(\frac{\alpha}{1+\xi}\right)}$, and the indirect utility function, V :

$$V = E\left\{p_A \left(1 - t\right)^\Phi + w \left(1 + r\right) \left(1 - t\right)^\Omega\right\} \tag{6.42}$$

where:

$$E = \frac{D^{\left(\frac{1+\xi}{1+\xi+\alpha}\right)} \left(1 + \delta\right)}{\left(1 + r\right)} \tag{6.43}$$

with:

$$D = \alpha^\alpha \left(\frac{1 - \alpha}{w \left(1 + \delta\right)}\right)^{(1-\alpha)} \frac{\alpha \left(1 + \xi\right)}{\left(1 + \alpha + \xi\right)} \left(\frac{\alpha \left(1 + r\right)}{\left(1 + \alpha + \xi\right)}\right)^{\left(\frac{\alpha}{1+\xi}\right)} \tag{6.44}$$

and:

$$\Phi = -\frac{\left(1 + \xi\right) \left(1 - \alpha\right)}{1 + \xi + \alpha} \tag{6.45}$$

$$\Omega = \frac{\alpha \left(2 + \xi\right)}{1 + \xi + \alpha} \tag{6.46}$$

In order to maximize V with respect to p_A and t, subject to the constraint (6.38) form the Lagrangean:

$$\mathcal{L} = V + \lambda \left[At^2 + \{(B - C) p_A - A\} t + C p_A\right] \tag{6.47}$$

The first-order conditions are, in addition to (6.38):

$$\frac{\partial \mathcal{L}}{\partial p_A} = E \left(1 - t\right)^\Phi + \lambda \{t \left(B - C\right) + I\} = 0 \tag{6.48}$$

$$\frac{\partial \mathcal{L}}{\partial t} = -E \left\{p_A \Phi \left(1 - t\right)^{\Phi - 1} + \Omega w \left(1 + r\right) \left(1 - t\right)^{\Omega - 1}\right\}$$

$$+ \quad \lambda \{A \left(2t - 1\right) + p_A \left(B - C\right)\} = 0 \tag{6.49}$$

From (6.38) express p_A as a function of t to give:

$$p_A = \frac{At \left(1 - t\right)}{Bt + C \left(1 - t\right)} \tag{6.50}$$

By substituting (6.50) into equation (6.49) and rearranging, λ can be expressed as a function of t: substituting this into equation (6.48) gives an equation determining the optimal tax rate. After a little rearranging, the optimal rate is found to be the root of:

$$1 + \left\{ \frac{Bt + C\left(1 - t\right)}{(B - C)\,t^2 + C\left(2t - 1\right)} \right\} \left[\Phi t + \{Bt + C\left(1 - t\right)\} \frac{\Omega w\left(1 + r\right)}{A} \right] = 0$$

(6.51)

This result can be used to calculate the optimal tax rate for a given set of parameters. But it can also be used to examine the relationship between r, δ and ρ that is required to support a given optimal tax rate. First, consider the locus of values such that the optimal tax rate is zero, whereby private saving alone is optimal and there is no role for social transfers between generations. Setting t in (6.51) equal to 0 gives:

$$A = \Omega C w\left(1 + r\right)$$

(6.52)

Expanding and rearranging (6.52), gives:

$$\delta + \rho + \delta\rho = r$$

(6.53)

Hence, when labour supplies are variable, the condition under which a pay-as-you-go pension scheme is optimal is exactly the same as in the model in which labour supplies are assumed to be fixed independently of the tax structure. The crucial ingredient in generating this result is the assumption that $p_B = p_A\left(1 + \delta\right)$, such that cohort B expects to receive a pension equal to the pension that it provides for cohort A, adjusted for the growth of real wages.

Figure 6.1 shows the values of δ required for given values of ρ, in order for the optimal tax rate to take the values of 0, 0.1 and 0.2. These values are for $r = 0.3$, $\xi = 0.3$, $w = 2$ and $\alpha = 0.7$. The locus of values for optimal $t = 0$ is of course taken from (6.53) and is independent of the other parameters of the model. The figure shows the extent to which δ must be higher in order to justify a higher optimal tax rate. Lower values of α imply a higher preference

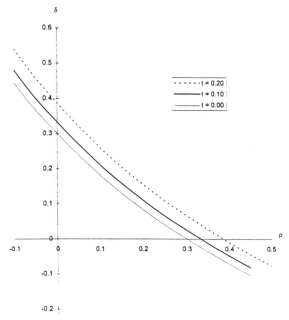

Figure 6.1: Variations in δ and ρ for given t

for leisure relative to consumption financed from net earnings; hence the rate of productivity growth, δ, required to support any positive optimal tax rate is higher. A higher value of the time preference rate, ξ, implies that present consumption is valued relatively more highly than future consumption; hence the value of δ required to support any given tax rate must also be higher. However, the outward shift in the profiles of Figure 6.1 is relatively small for variations in ξ compared with variations in α.

6.4 Conclusions

This chapter has extended the basic overlapping generations model that is typically used to examine the rationale for some types of pay-as-you-go pension systems. First, the framework was extended to allow for the case where some individuals in each cohort live longer. This uses a three-period model in which different generations of retired persons are alive at the same time and may be given a different pension. Secondly, allowance was made for labour supply responses to taxation whereby an attempt to raise revenue in order to finance current pensions introduces distortions into labour supply and a reduction in the tax base. The optimal tax rate was derived and the conditions under which the Samuelson-Aaron condition is unchanged were examined. The condition provides combinations of productivity and population growth and real interest rates for which the optimal tax rate is zero. In addition, productivity growth rates required in order to support alternative optimal tax rates were examined.

Chapter 7

Pensions and Contracting Out

The previous chapter examined the conditions under which the use of social transfers between generations is preferred to the use of private saving for retirement. An overlapping generations framework was used in which all members of the same cohort were assumed to be identical. Other arguments for the use of a government pension scheme have been based on quite different types of consideration. The present chapter discusses some aspects of state pensions that are related to insurance issues; on the rationale for state pensions, see also Creedy and Disney (1985). Emphasis is therefore given to differences between individuals, and the analysis is restricted to a single cohort, thereby abstracting from the types of issue discussed in chapter 6.

One argument for the use of a government pension scheme is that there is a market failure in the provision of private insurance. This is examined in section 7.1. The use of a government pension scheme involving *ex ante* redistribution within the cohort is then examined in section 7.2. In particular, the problems arising from contracting-out of a government scheme are considered.

7.1 Market Failure

7.1.1 Risk Pooling

The simplest example of a mechanism to deal with uncertainty at the individual level is that of risk pooling. Suppose there are n individuals, and each person faces an uncertain income, y_i, with $V(y) = \sigma_y^2$. The arrangement is that each person places income into a common pool, which is then divided equally among the members, so that each person receives the arithmetic mean, $\bar{y}$. The variance of total income is:

$$V\left(\sum_{i=1}^{n} y_i\right) = \sum_{i=1}^{n} V(y_i) = n\sigma_y^2 \tag{7.1}$$

A crucial assumption used in deriving (7.1) is that the risks are independent; hence the variances are additive. Pooling has no effect on the variance of total income. But the variance of each individual's income from risk pooling is the variance of $\bar{y}$, which is equal to:

$$\begin{aligned} V\left(\sum y_i/n\right) &= \sum V(y_i/n) \\ &= \sum \sigma_y^2/n^2 \\ &= \sigma_y^2/n \end{aligned} \tag{7.2}$$

This uses the general result that if a variable x has mean μ_x and variance σ_x^2, then $a + bx$ has mean $a + b\mu_x$ and variance $b^2\sigma_x^2$. Equation (7.2) shows that as the size of the pool increases the risk facing each individual is reduced; as $n \to \infty$ the individual risk is eliminated.

Risk pooling is thus a good arrangement for reducing individual risks in the special case where risks are independent. This explains to some extent the popularity of Friendly Societies in th UK in the nineteenth century. However, there are notable cases where the assumption breaks down; examples include the probability of flooding for individuals living in the same valley, the probability of damage during wars, the probability of becoming unemployed for individuals in the same occupation or firm, and the probability of catching a highly contagious disease. These risks cannot be diversified, and there are therefore grounds for thinking that markets may not be able to handle such risks. It has been argued that governments should provide insurance in these cases.

7.1.2 Market Failure and Self Selection

An important point to stress about the above system of risk pooling is that there is no redistribution of income among individuals from an *ex ante* point of view. This is because all individuals are assumed to face the same risk of loss. There is some redistribution *ex post*, but this is acceptable to members of the pool who have no incentive to leave (and the contract is assumed to be binding).

When there is population heterogeneity the market response is not so straightforward. Suppose that the heterogeneity is combined with asymmetric information. Hence individuals have information about their risks which is not available to insurance companies, perhaps because the costs of screening individuals is prohibitively high. If an insurance company bases its premium on the observed average risk, there is some redistribution from low- to high-risk individuals. In such a situation the low-risk individuals, who know they are low-risk but cannot convince the insurance company, may find that they are better off by engaging in self insurance. This includes activities such as saving and fitting security systems to property.

The low-risk individuals will therefore not purchase insurance, so the average risk of the remaining members will necessarily increase and the company will have to raise its premium. This leads to a further group of relatively low-risk individuals finding that they are better off by leaving the company and self-insuring. This process continues until only the highest-risk individual remains. This type of process, which essentially arises from the population heterogeneity combined with asymmetric information, is called 'self selection'. It can clearly lead to market failure; that is, a failure of the market to provide insurance for some high-risk individuals (those left after the low-risk people have 'selected out' of the market).

A possibility of avoiding this problem arises when the insurance company can find a suitable way of gaining information about risks. This may be done using coinsurance, where an individual pays a proportion of the cost (which is common in medical insurance), or deductibles, where the individual self insures for the first specified amount of cost (as commonly used in motor insurance or household contents insurance). Deductibles and coinsurance provide alternative contracts that are attractive to those who know they face low risks; they lead to what is known as a separating equilibrium whereby individuals, through self-selection, divide themselves into distinct groups.

7.2 A Government Pension Scheme

It has been seen that private market failure may arise if there are severe problems of self selection or when the risks cannot be diversified. The question then arises of whether government schemes can overcome these problems. It is through the use of compulsion that the state can operate insurance contracts that would not exist in private markets. This is discussed in this section in the context of a simple model of a fully funded state pension scheme.

7.2.1 A Two-period Model

In order to concentrate on the self-selection aspect of a fully funded state pension it is useful to consider a basic two-period framework. The first period is the 'working life' while the second period is 'retirement'. Suppose first that pensions and contributions are directly proportional to earnings. Then for the ith individual with earnings of y_i, pensions $P(y_i)$ and contributions $C(y_i)$ are simply:

$$P(y_i) = py_i \tag{7.3}$$

$$C(y_i) = cy_i \tag{7.4}$$

If there are n individuals and average earnings are denoted $\bar{y}$, then total contributions are $nc\bar{y}$ and total pension payments are $np\bar{y}$. The pension scheme is assumed to be fully funded, so that pensions are financed wholly from accumulated contributions, in contrast with a pay-as-you-go scheme. If the rate of interest earned by the pension fund is r, then:

$$nc\bar{y}(1+r) = np\bar{y} \tag{7.5}$$

and:

$$p = c(1+r) \tag{7.6}$$

Equation (7.6) gives the proportional pension rate that can be financed with any given contributions rate. Let r_i denote the rate of return obtained by the ith number of the scheme. This is given by:

$$(1+r_i) = \frac{P(y_i)}{C(y_i)} \tag{7.7}$$

Hence substituting (7.4) and (7.6) into (7.7) gives

$$(1+r_i) = c(1+r)\left(\frac{y_i}{cy_i}\right) = 1+r \tag{7.8}$$

and each person receives the same rate of return as obtained by the fund in the market. Hence there is no redistribution and no one has any incentive to leave the scheme (assuming that c is not so high as to involve compulsory 'oversaving').

Now suppose that there is a flat-rate pension, b, received by all individuals irrespective of their contributions. If this is combined with proportional contributions, there is clearly some redistribution; the scheme is equivalent to a linear income tax. For the scheme to be self-financing:

$$nb = nc\bar{y}(1+r) \tag{7.9}$$

and

$$b = \bar{y}c(1+r) \tag{7.10}$$

Substitution into (7.7) gives:

$$1+r_i = (1+r)\left(\frac{\bar{y}}{y_i}\right) \tag{7.11}$$

Hence those with $y_i > \bar{y}$ obtain a rate of return that is less than the rate, r, obtained by the fund. They therefore have a strong incentive to leave the scheme. The process of self-selection would eventually produce a scheme with only the poorest person in it. In order to avoid this problem, a government could, as suggested earlier, make membership compulsory.

7.2.2   Contracting Out of the State Scheme

Instead of making membership of the pension compulsory, the government could allow 'contracting out' but impose a 'penalty' by making individuals who contract out leave a proportion, δ, of their contributions in the state fund. The effect of such an arrangement is to reduce the effective rate of return obtained in the market by a contracting-out person to $1-(1-\delta)(1+r)$ rather than r. This restricts the incentive to contract out. Contracting out has been an important feature of government pension schemes in the UK, particularly in the context of the state earnings-related pension.

Contracting out can be illustrated by the following numerical example using only 10 individuals. The hypothetical individuals and their incomes during the working life are shown in Table 7.1. The incomes are listed in ascending order. The last two columns give the proportion of total income obtained by those with incomes less than or equal to a given amount, $F_1(y)$, and the corresponding proportion of people, $F(y)$. These are respectively the first moment distribution function and the distribution function; they therefore provide the information required for plotting the well-known Lorenz curve. Arithmetic mean income, $\bar{y}$, is 425.

Consider the fourth row of the table: the last two entries in this row indicate that 20 per cent of the total income is earned by 40 per cent of the people. Similarly the fifth line indicates that half the people obtain only 28.2 per cent of the total income.

Suppose that the contributions rate, c, is 0.15 and the rate of interest, r, is 0.50. Although r appears to be very high, it is appropriate for this kind of model where the lifetime is condensed into two periods. Total accumulated contributions, of $(0.15)(4,250)$ plus the interest, must be equal to total pension payments in order for the scheme to be self-financing. Hence:

$$0.15(4250)(1.5) = 10b \qquad (7.12)$$

and the flat-rate pension is:

$$b = 95.63 \qquad (7.13)$$

Suppose that contracted-out people have to leave a proportion, $\delta = 0.30$,

Table 7.1: Hypothetical Income Distribution

Person number	Income y_i	Total income	$F_1(y)$	$F(y)$
1	100	100	0.024	0.1
2	200	300	0.071	0.2
3	250	550	0.129	0.3
4	300	850	0.200	0.4
5	350	1200	0.282	0.5
6	350	1550	0.365	0.6
7	400	1950	0.459	0.7
8	500	2450	0.576	0.8
9	800	3250	0.765	0.9
10	1000	4250	1.000	1.0

of their contributions in the state fund. This reduces their effective rate of return from private saving, r^e, such that:

$$
\begin{aligned}
1 + r^e &= (1 - \delta)(1 + r) = (0.70)(1.5) \\
&= 1.05
\end{aligned}
\tag{7.14}
$$

But if the basic pension is 95.63, the richest person has an implied rate of return from the scheme of r_{10}, where

$$
\begin{aligned}
1 + r_{10} &= 95.63/(0.15)(1000) \\
&= 0.64
\end{aligned}
\tag{7.15}
$$

This is considerably less than $1 + r^e = 1.05$, so the richest person has a strong incentive to contract out. If the richest person leaves, the basic pension is reduced. Its new value is given by:

$$
0.15\{3250 - 0.3(1000)\}(1.5) = 9b
\tag{7.16}
$$

and:

$$
b = 88.75
\tag{7.17}
$$

Now consider the richest person remaining in the scheme, the ninth person in Table 7.1. The rate of return obtained by this person from the scheme, r_9, is given by:

$$1 + r_9 = 88.75/(0.15)(800) \qquad (7.18)$$
$$= 0.74$$

This rate of return is considerably less than the return from private saving of 1.05; hence the ninth person also has an incentive to contract out. With eight people remaining, the basic pension falls further. The budget constraint is:

$$0.15\{2450 + 0.3(1800)\}(1.5) = 8b \qquad (7.19)$$

and the flat-rate pension falls to:

$$b = 84.10 \qquad (7.20)$$

Consider the richest person still remaining in the scheme, person number 7. The implied rate of return from the state scheme is given by:

$$1 + r_7 = 84.10/(0.15)(500)$$
$$= 1.12 \qquad (7.21)$$

which exceeds 1.05, the effective market return for contracted-out individuals. Hence person number 7 has no incentive to leave. This means that the system is stable with eight members and two people contracting out. It can be seen that a reduction in δ would increase the number of people who have an incentive to contract out.

7.2.3 A Formal Statement

The procedure can be described formally for the general case as follows. Define y^* as the income above which individuals contract out; this may be called the contracting-out margin. Two equations are relevant. The first is used to determine the basic pension that can be paid to those in the system. This is:

$$Nc\left\{\int_0^{y^*} ydF(y) + \delta\int_{y^*}^{\infty} ydF(y)\right\}(1+r) = Nb\int_0^{y^*} dF(y) \tag{7.22}$$

The first term on the left-hand side of equation (7.22) represents the accumulated contributions of the members of the scheme. The second term on the left-hand side gives the accumulated contributions made by those who contract out of the scheme. The right-hand side represents the total pension payments requred for the members. This expression can be reduced to:

$$c\bar{y}\left[F_1(y^*) + \delta\{1 - F_1(y^*)\}\right](1+r) = bF(y^*) \tag{7.23}$$

where F_1 has been defined above; on the use of this type of manipulation, see Creedy (1996) and chapter 8 below.

The second equation required states that the rate of return at the contracting out margin, r^*, is equal to the effective market rate of return. Hence:

$$1 + r^* = \frac{b}{cy^*} = (1-\delta)(1+r) \tag{7.24}$$

Equations (7.23) and (7.24) can be solved for δ and y^*, given values of c, r and knowledge of the distribution of income. It can be shown that:

$$\frac{\delta}{1-\delta} = \left(\frac{y^*}{\bar{y}}\right)F(y^*) - F_1(y^*) \tag{7.25}$$

For example, it is easily checked that equation (7.25) conforms with the above numerical example. Take a value of y^* of 500. Then using the values in Table 7.1 it is found that:

$$\begin{aligned}\delta/(1-\delta) &= (0.8)(500/425) - 0.576 \\ &= 0.365\end{aligned} \tag{7.26}$$

Hence solving for δ gives:

$$\delta = 0.365/1.365 = 0.27 \tag{7.27}$$

Remember that in the above example, in which δ was set to 0.30, the eighth person was found to be just inside the margin. More complex schemes may be examined using the same basic approach although of course the algebra becomes more difficult; see Creedy (1982).

7.3   Conclusions

This chapter has shown how self-selection can produce a market failure in insurance, where there is asymmetric information combined with population heterogeneity. This can be overcome by governments operating a compulsory scheme, using their power to tax. In such cases, where *ex ante* redistribution arises, an alternative is to allow individuals to contract out of a state scheme, provided that a proportion of their contributions remains in the scheme. It is shown that this can produce a stable situation in which a proportion of the richest individuals contract out.

Chapter 8

Two-tier State Pensions

This chapter is concerned with the role of state pension schemes in redistributing lifetime income within a single cohort of individuals. As suggested by Atkinson (1987, p.810), 'the redistribution of lifetime income *between individuals* may be a major objective' of a state pension scheme. Using a two-period model, Atkinson contrasts a simple scheme involving proportional (earnings-related) contributions and proportional pensions, which involves no redistribution, with a scheme giving a uniform flat-rate pension. The latter is of course progressive and 'the desirability of such a "tilt" in the benefit formula would depend on the distributional objectives pursued' (1987, p.810).

In practice, state pensions often involve some combination of flat-rate and earnings-related pension benefits. For example, the UK state scheme has a basic pension combined with a second tier which is proportional to the difference between pensionable earnings and the basic pension. The non-linear nature of such a benefit formula implies that replacement rates fall with income, so that the extent of the redistribution involved lies somewhere between the simple earnings-related scheme and the flat-rate pension.

If it is assumed that earnings remain fixed irrespective of the pension and tax system, analysis of the nature of the policy trade-offs in alternative schemes is fairly straightforward. Comparisons were made in Creedy (1982) using a two-period model in which the first period corresponds to the working life and the second period corresponds to retirement. This chapter extends that analysis by allowing for labour supply responses, and adding transfer payments in the first (working) period. The labour supply effects of alternative schemes would be expected to differ significantly; in particular a higher proportional pension rate in an earnings-related scheme such as that operating in the UK would be expected to be associated with a higher labour supply, *ceteris paribus*. This may be expected to change the nature of the trade-off between equity and efficiency in alternative schemes. In the present context this trade-off can be examined in terms of a measure of inequality of lifetime utility and the value of a social welfare function specified in terms of individual utilities.

The basic model is presented in section 8.1, which derives the labour supply function and the government budget constraint. The latter is non-linear and requires numerical methods for its solution. Section 8.2 goes on to examine the relationship between pension structures and the required tax rate, along with the trade-off between equity and efficiency implied by the use of a social welfare function specified in terms of individuals' utilities. For consistency, Atkinson's (1970) measure of inequality is used in combination with the well-known iso-elastic welfare function.

8.1   The Two-period Model

8.1.1   Earnings-related Pensions and Labour Supply

The basic model involves a single cohort of individuals within a two-period framework. Individuals can work only in the first period and retire in the second period. The proportion of time devoted to labour supply in the first period is equal to $1 - h$, with $h \leq 1$, and consumption expenditure is c_1 and c_2 in the first and second periods respectively. Define the time preference rate as ξ, with $\theta = 1/(1 + \xi)$, and suppose that the lifetime utility function can be written in logarithmic form as:

$$\log (U) = \log (c_1^\alpha) + \log \left(h^{1-\alpha}\right) + \theta \log (c_2^\alpha) \tag{8.1}$$

This can be regarded as the monotonic transformation of the following Cobb-Douglas utility function with three goods:

$$U = c_1^\alpha h^{1-\alpha} c_2^{\alpha\theta} \tag{8.2}$$

Suppose, in addition, that there is a government pension scheme of the two-tier variety. Individuals whose earnings during the first period are below a basic pension, b, receive only the basic pension. For simplicity, all individuals are regarded as being eligible for the basic pension. Those whose earnings exceed b receive an additional or second-tier pension equal to a proportion, s, of earnings measured above b. Hence if the wage rate facing an individual is denoted by w, earnings are given by $w(1-h)$ and the pension, p, is equal to:

$$
\begin{aligned}
p &= b & \text{for } w(1-h) \le b \tag{8.3} \\
&= b + s\left\{w(1-h) - b\right\} & \text{for } w(1-h) > b \tag{8.4}
\end{aligned}
$$

Suppose that the pension is financed using a proportional tax or contribution system, where t represents the fixed marginal and average tax rate. The tax system can also be assumed to finance an unconditional transfer, equal to a, to each individual during the first period; a special case would involve $a = b$. Suppose each individual is able to borrow and lend at the fixed rate of interest, r. For those whose earnings exceed the basic pension, the lifetime budget constraint can therefore be written as:

$$c_1 + \frac{c_2}{(1+r)} = a + \frac{b(1-s)}{(1+r)} + w(1-h)\left\{1 - t + \frac{s}{(1+r)}\right\} \tag{8.5}$$

This can be modified for the situation where the individual works but does not qualify for the second-tier pension, by setting $s = 0$. The constraint in (8.5) not only assumes perfect capital markets but also ignores the possibility of interest-income taxation. The latter would reduce the after-tax rate of return for those who lend in the first period to $r(1-t)$ and introduces a further kink in the budget constraint, but otherwise has no effect on the comparisons among pension schemes and is ignored here.

The specification of the lifetime utility function as a type of multi-good Cobb-Douglas function makes the derivation of interior solutions particularly straightforward. For example, it is well-known that maximisation of $\sum_i \alpha_i \log c_i$ subject to the constraint that $\sum_i p_i c_i = W$ gives solutions of the form $c_i = \{\alpha_i / (\sum_i \alpha_i)\} (W/p_i)$, and thus linear expenditure functions. In the present context, the corresponding 'price' of consumption in the first and second periods respectively is 1 and $1/(1+r)$, while the sum of the exponents is simply $1 + \alpha\theta$. Here, where labour supply is endogenous, W must be interpreted as 'full income'; that is, W is the maximum after-tax income that could be obtained if no leisure were consumed. Similarly, the 'price' of leisure is equal to the appropriate value of the after-tax wage rate.

The existence of the two-tier pension scheme means that two types of interior solution must be distinguished. First, for those working but not qualifying for the earnings-related pension, the post-tax wage rate, from (8.5) with $s = 0$, is $w(1-t)$, while full income, W is:

$$a + \frac{b}{(1+r)} + w(1-t) \tag{8.6}$$

For those who qualify for the earnings-related component, the post-tax wage rate is equal to $w\{1 - t + s/(1+r)\}$ and full income is:

$$a + \frac{b(1-s)}{(1+r)} + w\left\{1 - t + \frac{s}{(1+r)}\right\} \tag{8.7}$$

Consumption in each period may therefore be written as:

$$c_1 = \left\{\frac{\alpha}{(1+\alpha\theta)}\right\} W \tag{8.8}$$

$$c_2 = \left\{\frac{\alpha\theta}{(1+\alpha\theta)}\right\} W(1+r) \tag{8.9}$$

with the appropriate value of W in each case. Leisure is equal to

$$h = \frac{\{(1-\alpha)/(1+\alpha\theta)\} W}{w(1-t)} \tag{8.10}$$

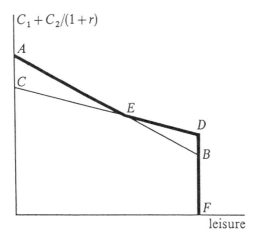

Figure 8.1: The Budget Constraint

if only the basic pension is received, and is

$$h = \frac{\{(1 - \alpha)/(1 + \alpha\theta)\} W}{w \{1 - t + s/(1 + r)\}} \tag{8.11}$$

if the individual qualifies for the second-tier pension. The labour supply incentive provided by the earnings-related pension is seen directly from the effective reduction in the marginal tax rate which is implied.

Special care must, however, be taken in dealing with corner solutions in this model. The simplest case is where it is not worthwhile supplying any labour if the resulting earnings only qualify the individual for a basic pension; that is if $w(1 - h) \leq b$. Appropriate substitution into (8.10) and rearrangement shows that for $h < 1$ the wage must exceed w_L, where:

$$w_L = \frac{(1 - \alpha) \{a + b/(1 + r)\}}{\alpha (1 + \theta) (1 - t)} \tag{8.12}$$

However, the situation is complicated by the fact that the budget constraint is non-convex. This is most easily seen by examining (8.5) for the two cases where $s = 0$ and $s > 0$, as illustrated in Figure 8.1. The effective constraint is the kinked line AEDF. This is very similar to the type of two-rate single-period tax and transfer scheme examined by Lambert (1985,

1988, 1990) and Creedy (1996). Lambert stressed that the whole of the range of the constraint, corresponding to the length AED, is not relevant because there are some wage rates at which the individual switches, or jumps, from the flatter to the steeper section. This occurs when an indifference curve is tangential to both sections. For a simultaneous tangency along both sections, it is necessary to have, where primes indicate values along the flatter section (flat-rate pension only is received):

$$\left(\frac{c_1}{c_1'}\right)^\alpha \left(\frac{c_2}{c_2'}\right)^{\alpha\theta} \left(\frac{h}{h'}\right)^{1-\alpha} = 1 \tag{8.13}$$

Using the results in (8.8) to (8.11), substitution into (8.13) gives

$$\left(\frac{W}{W'}\right)^{1+\alpha\theta} \left\{\frac{1-t}{1-t+s/(1+r)}\right\}^{1-\alpha} = 1 \tag{8.14}$$

where

$$W' = a + \frac{b}{(1+r)} + w(1-t) \tag{8.15}$$

and

$$W = a + \frac{b(1-s)}{(1+r)} + w\left\{1-t+\frac{s}{(1+r)}\right\} \tag{8.16}$$

Hence:

$$W = kW' \tag{8.17}$$

where

$$k = \left\{1 + \frac{s}{(1-t)(1+r)}\right\}^{(1-\alpha)/(1+\alpha\theta)} \tag{8.18}$$

It is therefore possible to solve (8.17) to find the value of w, w_s say, at which the switching between segments occurs, whereby:

$$w_s = \frac{\{a+b/(1+r)\}(k-1)+bs/(1+r)}{(1-t)(1-k)+s/(1+r)} \tag{8.19}$$

The possibility also arises that, for high tax rates, the value of w_s in (8.19) is less than w_L in (8.12). This means that the tangency along the flatter range of the budget constraint in Figure 8.1 occurs beyond the relevant range (that is, it occurs where $h > 1$), so that it is never worthwhile working unless the individual qualifies for the earnings-related component of the state pension. The implications of this possibility will be discussed further below.

8.1.2 The Government Budget Constraint

Both the income transfer and the state pension must be financed within the present model from income taxation. Most state pensions are financed on a pay-as-you-go basis whereby the current pensions are financed from taxes paid by the current labour force. The existence of productivity and population growth gives individuals a higher effective rate of return from membership of the state scheme than the rate of return which could be achieved in the market; this is the basis of the analysis of chapter 6. Allowances for population and other changes could be made within the framework, but in the present context, where concentration is on distributional comparisons among alternative state pension schemes, it is most appropriate to concentrate on steady-state results in which no inter-cohort redistribution takes place. Kennedy (1990) has argued that the distributional implications of pensions should be examined in the context of a single cohort with deficit neutrality imposed. Thus, any effects of inter-generational transfers should be excluded.

As a single cohort is being considered, the present value of transfers plus pensions must equal the total tax revenue obtained during the working period. Interest-income taxation is excluded and the pension is non-taxable, so there is no government revenue in the second period. Capital markets have been assumed to be perfect, so the government's discount rate is the same as that at which individuals borrow and lend. The present approach also ignores deaths during the earlier period by assuming that all individuals live until the end of the second period.

The present value of flat-rate benefits per person in the cohort is $a+b/(1+r)$. The total earnings-related pensions received during the second period depends on the distribution of earnings, in combination with the pension formula. In principle, it would be possible to suppose that individuals not only face different wage rates, but also have different preferences in terms of their values of α and θ. However, it would be rather awkward to deal with such a joint distribution, and not surprisingly the literature on labour supply typically assumes simply that individuals differ in the wage rate faced. Suppose, then, that the distribution function of w is represented by $F(w)$. Total earnings-related pensions per person are therefore given by:

$$s \int_{w_s}^{\infty} \{w(1-h) - b\} \, dF(w) \tag{8.20}$$

It is most convenient to use (8.11) to express earnings $w(1-h)$ in terms of w and the parameters of the tax and transfer system, as:

$$w(1-h) = \alpha^* w - \psi \tag{8.21}$$

with:

$$\alpha^* = \alpha(1+\theta)/(1+\alpha\theta) \tag{8.22}$$

and:

$$\psi = \frac{(1-\alpha)\{a + b(1-s)/(1+r)\}}{(1+\alpha\theta)\{1 - t + s/(1+r)\}} \tag{8.23}$$

Equation (8.21) gives the familiar looking result (from the single period Cobb-Douglas models of a linear income tax) that earnings are a linear function of the wage rate, above a threshold value.

Substituting in (8.20) and rearranging gives total earnings-related pensions per person as the proportional pension rate, s, multiplied by:

$$\alpha^* \overline{w} \{1 - F_1(w_s)\} - (\psi + b)\{1 - F(w_s)\} \tag{8.24}$$

where $\overline{w}$ is the arithmetic mean value of w and $F_1(w_s)$ denotes the proportion of total income obtained by those with incomes not exceeding w_s; hence F_1 denotes the 'incomplete first moment' distribution function of F.

The final stage involved in specifying the budget constraint is to obtain the income tax base, since the tax system is proportional. For those working in the first period, but earning insufficient to qualify for an earnings-related pension, it is convenient to use (8.22) to write gross earnings as:

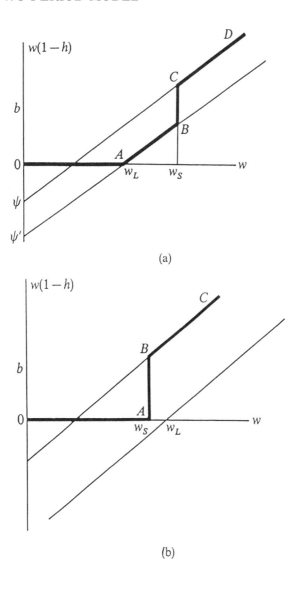

Figure 8.2: Labour Supply and the Wage Rate

$$w(1 - h) = \alpha w - \psi' \tag{8.25}$$

where ψ' is obtained from the right-hand side of (8.23) by setting $s = 0$. The labour supply function, relating $w(1 - h)$, or labour measured in 'efficiency units', to the wage rate is therefore the kinked line OABCD shown in Figure 8.2. For a wage between w_L and w_s the individual works but does not receive an earnings-related pension. As the wage reaches w_s the individual jumps from B to C and then follows the range CD. Part (a) of Figure 8.2 is drawn for $w_s > w_L$, which is the typical situation but, as mentioned above, this inequality can be reversed for very high tax rates. If $w_L > w_s$ then the function is illustrated in part (b) of Figure 8.2 where earnings jump from zero to B at w_s; notice that the earnings corresponding to w_s must exceed the basic pension.

If $w_s > w_L$, the tax base is equal to the number of individuals in the cohort multiplied by:

$$\int_{w_L}^{w_s} (\alpha^* w - \psi') \, dF(w) + \int_{w_s}^{\infty} (\alpha^* w - \psi) \, dF(w) \tag{8.26}$$

This can be rearranged to give:

$$\alpha^* \int_{w_L}^{\infty} w \, dF(w) - \left\{ \psi' \int_{w_L}^{w_s} dF(w) + \psi \int_{w_s}^{w_\infty} dF(w) \right\} \tag{8.27}$$

Further simplification using the first moment distribution function gives the expression:

$$\alpha^* \overline{w} \left\{ 1 - F_1(w_L) \right\} - \psi' \left\{ F(w_s) - F(w_L) \right\} - \psi \left\{ 1 - F(w_s) \right\}$$

The tax rate, t, needed to finance any specified pension scheme, after allowing for labour supply responses, is given by:

$$t = \frac{a + [b + s[\alpha^* \overline{w} \{1 - F_1(w_s)\} - (\psi + b)\{1 - F(w_s)\}]]/(1 + r)}{\alpha^* \overline{w} \{1 - F_1(w_L)\} - \psi' \{F(w_s) - F(w_L)\} - \psi \{1 - F(w_s)\}} \tag{8.28}$$

In the case where $w_L > w_s$, it can be seen that the denomination of (8.28) is changed to:

$$\alpha^* \overline{w} \left\{ 1 - F_1 \left(w_s \right) \right\} - \psi \left\{ F \left(w_s \right) \right\} \tag{8.29}$$

However, equation (8.28) is deceptively 'simple' because the various terms on the right-hand side, such as ψ, ψ', w_s and w_L, all depend on t. The budget constraint can therefore only be solved using numerical methods. It is, however, useful to consider a special case of (8.28) where all individuals qualify for the earnings-related pension; this arises if the minimum wage rate is sufficiently high, given the other parameters. Hence $F \left(w_L \right) = F \left(w_s \right) = F_1 \left(w_L \right) = F_1 \left(w_s \right) = 0$ and (8.28) reduces to:

$$t = \frac{a + \left\{ b + s \left(\alpha^* \overline{w} - \psi - b \right) \right\} / \left(1 + r \right)}{\alpha^* \overline{w} - \psi} \tag{8.30}$$

This result has a simple interpretation: the required tax rate is the present value of the benefits received by someone with the arithmetic mean wage rate, $\overline{w}$, divided by the corresponding gross earnings. Even this intuitively obvious expression for the tax rate in this special case cannot be solved easily since ψ depends on t.

The government budget constraint may be solved using the following iterative numerical procedure. First, despite the way in which (8.28) has been expressed, it is not appropriate to attempt to solve for t, given a specified value of the basic pension, b. This is because t is not uniquely defined for given b. Thus, start by selecting a value of t, along with an arbitrary initial value of b, and then evaluate the right-hand side of equation (8.28). If the resulting value exceeds the chosen tax rate, select a slightly lower value of the basic pension and repeat the calculation until a value of b is found for which the right-hand side of (8.28) is the selected tax rate.

The evaluation of (8.28) requires the assumption of an explicit functional form for the distribution function $F(w)$. It is assumed below that wage rates are lognormally distributed as $\Lambda \left(w | \mu, \sigma^2 \right)$, for which the first moment distribution, $F_1(w)$, is readily obtained from the general result that $\Lambda_1 \left(w | \mu, \sigma^2 \right) = \Lambda \left(w | \mu + \sigma, \sigma^2 \right)$; see Aitchison and Brown (1957). The integrals in (8.28) can be obtained using a polynomial approximation to the integrals of the standard normal distribution and the fact that $\log(w)$ is

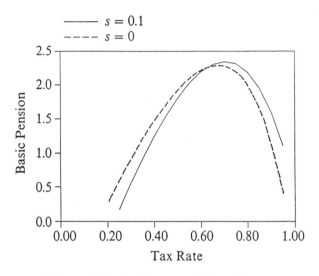

Figure 8.3: Tax Rate and Basic Pension

$N(\mu, \sigma^2)$.

8.1.3   Tax and Benefit Levels

The procedure described above for solving the government's budget constraint was applied in order to produce the results shown in Figure 8.3. The precise units in which incomes and transfers are measured are not relevant, and values of μ and σ^2 were set at 1.8 and 0.3 respectively, with the first period transfer, a, set at 0.8. In two-period models of this kind it is appropriate to set the rates of interest and time preference quite high (although the absolute values do not affect the comparisons between alternative schemes), and these were set at 0.5 and 0.7 respectively. The value of α was 0.65. It is important to stress that these values were chosen for illustrative purposes only; the comparisons are not affected by specific values.

Figure 8.3 shows how the basic pension can vary as the tax rate is increased, for two alternative values of the proportional pension rate, zero and 0.10. This type of schedule has been referred to, in different contexts, as a 'transfer possibility locus' by Atkinson (1987, p.798) or simply as a 'revenue constraint' by Atkinson and Stiglitz (1980, p.401). The figure shows that as the tax rate increases, the basic pension ultimately falls because of the decline in the tax base outweighing the rise in t. However, because of the labour supply incentive the decline is delayed when there is an earnings-related pension, compared with the flat-rate case. Hence with an earnings-related component, it is possible to obtain a higher basic pension than in a simple flat-rate scheme. Notice that the profiles do not begin at the point $b = a = 0$ because of the existence of the transfer payment during the working period. They would begin at the origin if $a = b$ at all times, but otherwise they have very similar shapes. To extend the tax rate beyond the peak of each profile in Figure 8.3 would involve reducing the income transfer to the poor while also making the relatively rich worse-off.

The concave nature of the transfer possibility loci contrasts with the case where no allowance is made for labour supply effects, as examined in Creedy (1982, p.27). In the latter case, the various schedules (for alternative values of s) are virtually parallel and do not turn downwards. For lower values of b in Figure 8.3 the relationship is steeper for higher values of s. This arises partly because when b increases, for given s, fewer members of the cohort are eligible for the earnings-related component of the pension; furthermore, for given b, labour supply increases with s.

It should be borne in mind that the present analysis is of a pure transfer scheme; all tax revenue is redistributed as transfers to members of the same cohort. Hence all redistribution takes place from those above the arithmetic mean earnings to those below. Despite the high values of t that may be implied, average tax rates for those below the mean are negative. This property incidentally allows a useful check on calculations, since the arithmetic mean values of gross and net lifetime income should be the same. Another way of stating this implication is to say that the rate of return to membership of the state transfer system is less than the market rate of interest for those with earnings above the arithmetic mean, and *vice versa*. But it is the precise variation in such rates of return which affects the extent of the redistribution involved, and this is considered in the next section.

8.2   Equity and Efficiency

In considering the choice between alternative transfer schemes when labour
supply responses occur, it seems most appropriate to examine explicitly the
trade-off between equity and efficiency. Further analysis requires the use of
explicit value judgements involving inter-personal comparisons. Such judgements are summarised by the form of social welfare function used. The government may be regarded as maximising a social welfare function, subject
to the constraint imposed by its revenue requirement, while each individual
maximises utility, subject to an individual budget constraint that depends on
the wage rate faced and the tax and transfer parameters chosen by the government. This is of course the standard optimal tax problem, now considered
in the context of a two-period model with a pension scheme.

The trade-off between equity and efficiency is explicit when using, for
example, the social welfare function implied by Atkinson's (1970) measure
of inequality, for alternative degrees of aversion to inequality. In the present
context, where the value placed on leisure by individuals is explicitly examined, it is most appropriate to consider the inequality of *utility*, rather than
simply net income. For given inequality aversion, Atkinson's measure defines
a set of indifference curves relating average utility to its inequality. Where
U_i denotes person i's lifetime utility, social welfare, W, is given by:

$$\begin{aligned} W &= \frac{1}{1-\varepsilon}\sum_i U_i^{1-\varepsilon} \qquad \text{for } \varepsilon \neq 1 \\ &= \sum_i \log U_i \qquad \text{for } \varepsilon = 1 \end{aligned} \qquad (8.31)$$

where ε reflects the degree of aversion to inequality. Atkinson's inequality
measure $I(\varepsilon)$, is defined as:

$$I(\varepsilon) = 1 - U_{ede}/\bar{U} \qquad (8.32)$$

where $\bar{U}$ and U_{ede} are respectively the arithmetic mean utility and the 'equally
distributed equivalent' level which, if enjoyed by each individual, would generate the same social welfare as the actual distribution. Equations (8.31) and
(8.32) can be combined to give welfare per person equal to:

$$\frac{\left[\bar{U}\left\{1 - I\left(\varepsilon\right)\right\}\right]^{1-\varepsilon}}{1 - \varepsilon} \tag{8.33}$$

so that indifference curves have the slope $d\bar{U}/dI = \bar{U}\left\{1 - I\left(\varepsilon\right)\right\}^{-1}$. It should be noted that although individual choices are not affected by the particular cardinalisation of utility functions (for example, either (8.1) or (8.2) above), the use of this type of social welfare function is affected by the form chosen. From (8.31) it can immediately be seen that the combination of (8.2) with $\varepsilon = 1$ leads to the same form of W as when (8.1) is combined with $\varepsilon = 0$. For this reason, results are obtained below for both cardinalisations.

The government's choice is represented by a tangency position of an indifference curve with a graph of average utility plotted against inequality (for a given value of ε). The latter represents the actual trade-off which is available between equity and efficiency in a given pension scheme. This relationship, along with the values of social welfare in alternative schemes, must be obtained numerically: given the non-linearity of the labour supply function, no convenient analytical expressions for the various terms are available. The approach involves obtaining a simulated 'population' of individuals, based on the assumed form of the wage rate distribution, $\Lambda\left(w|\mu, \sigma^2\right)$. The wage rate faced by the ith individual is calculated using a random number generator that gives a random drawing, v_i, from a standard normal distribution $N(0, 1)$. The ith person's wage rate, w_i, is then given by $w_i = \exp\left(\mu + v_i\sigma\right)$, which uses the fact that as w is lognormal, $(\log w - \mu)/\sigma$ follows a standard normal distribution. For given parameters of the model, the value of b corresponding to a specified tax rate, t, is obtained by solving (8.28) iteratively, as described earlier. Given the resulting value, it is then necessary to find the values of c_1, c_2 and h, and hence U, for each individual in the simulated population. This second stage gives the values of U_i, from which $I(\varepsilon)$, $\bar{U}$ and the value of social welfare, can be calculated. The procedure is then repeated for alternative values of t. All the results reported below are based on a simulated population of 10,000 individuals.

The trade-offs for flat rate and earnings-related schemes are shown in Figure 8.4, using the same parameters as for Figure 8.3. The profiles are for a

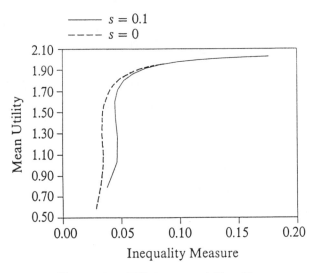

Figure 8.4: Efficiency and Equality

value of the inequality aversion parameter, ε, of 2 and the multiplicative form
of the utility function in (8.2). The vertical axis measures arithmetic mean
utility and the horizontal axis measures $I(\varepsilon)$. The indifference curves representing equal levels of social welfare per person, given above, slope upwards
from left to right and higher values of welfare are obtained on indifference
curves which are 'higher' when moving from the bottom right to the top
left-hand corner of the diagram.

The trade-offs in Figure 8.4 have a number of interesting features. First,
for both flat rate and two-tier schemes, they become very steep so that,
beyond a point, attempts to reduce inequality by raising the tax rate (and
hence the basic pension) involve large reductions in average utility. Indeed,
both profiles are non-concave over a range of values; just as an attempt to
increase the basic pension by raising the tax rate is eventually self-defeating,
inequality also rises slightly over a range. Non-concave trade-off relationships
have also been found by Lambert (1990), although he considered post-tax
and transfer income in a single-period context. The interesting similarity is
that Lambert also modelled a non-convex budget constraint, although the
situation discussed in Figure 8.4 cannot arise in his model.

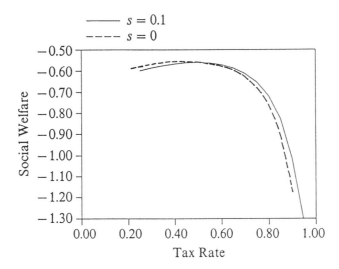

Figure 8.5: Tax Rate and Social Welfare

The second feature of Figure 8.4, and perhaps the most important result, is that the flat-rate pension scheme always dominates the two-tier scheme with an earnings related component, in that a higher value of social welfare can always be achieved. Despite the labour supply incentive provided by the earnings-related pension, the maximum social welfare achievable is less than the maximum attainable with only a flat rate pension. This result is also reflected in Figure 8.5, which shows social welfare in relation to the tax rate, for the two schemes. The profile for the flat-rate pension reaches a maximum at a lower tax rate than for the two-tier scheme, and although the profiles intersect, the peak of the former is higher than that of the latter. The values of social welfare are of course negative because of the term $1 - \varepsilon$ in the denominator.

It was mentioned above that the measure of social welfare depends on the particular cardinalisation of the utility function used although it is entirely arbitrary from the point of view of the individual's optimisation problem. For this reason the trade-off relationships were also obtained for the logarithmic form of equation (8.1). The results are shown in Figure 8.6. The most dramatic difference between Figures 8.4 and 8.6 is that the profiles in Figure

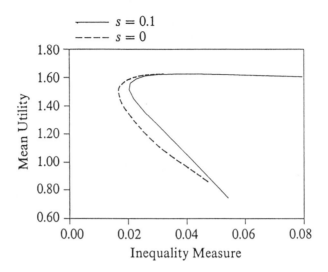

Figure 8.6: Efficiency and Equality

8.6 are strongly backward-bending over a range. Nevertheless, the major result that the flat-rate scheme dominates the two-tier scheme, allowing a higher social indifference curve to be reached, continues to hold.

It was suggested above that it is appropriate to measure social welfare in terms of individuals' utility levels, given the value placed on leisure in their utility functions. However, it is of interest to consider the implied trade-off between average net lifetime *income* and its inequality, particularly as incomes are the predominant focus of applied studies of inequality. Breit's (1974) statement of a general type of trade-off was also in terms of incomes rather than utilities. Results are shown in Figure 8.7, again using an inequality aversion parameter of $\varepsilon = 2$. A significant difference compared with the results in Figures 8.5 or 8.6 is that the trade-off profiles in Figure 8.7 do not have a backward-bending range. Hence, in this context it is possible for higher tax rates, beyond some value, to reduce the measured inequality of net income while simultaneously increasing the inequality of utility. This contrasts with the single-period results for a linear income tax, where inequality of net income and utility move in the same direction over the whole range of tax rates. The absence of a backward-bending range in Figure 8.7 should

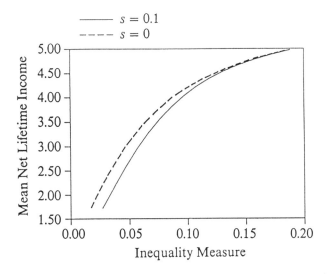

Figure 8.7: Efficiency and Equality

not, however, be thought to suggest that a social welfare function specified in terms of net incomes attains a maximum for a higher tax rate than that at which one specified in terms of utility reaches a maximum. Indeed, the reverse is true, so an emphasis on net incomes would produce a tax rate (and basic pension) that is in some sense too low.

It may be noted that the types of trade-off considered are entirely static in that any changes in average lifetime earnings are attributed purely to labour supply effects. There has been much debate on the effects of alternative pension schemes on savings. Aggregate savings in this model include both private savings and public savings measured by the excess of the tax revenue over the amount needed to finance the income transfer, a, given in the first period. For a given basic pension, it has been seen that the positive effect of increasing the proportional rate, s, on labour supply dominates the negative effect of the resulting increase in t, so labour supply increases in aggregate (it does not change for those at the corner solution with $w = w_L$ of course). It is also found that aggregate savings are higher with an earnings-related scheme than with just a flat-rate pension, for given values of b.

8.3   Conclusions

This chapter compared alternative state pension schemes using a two-period framework which allows for labour supply responses to changes in the tax and transfer structure. It was found that a two-tier pension scheme gives rise to a non-convex budget constraint facing individuals, leading to an interesting range of labour supply responses. An increase in the proportional pension rate used in the second tier (the earnings-related component) was found to increase aggregate labour supply, despite the rise in the tax rate needed to finance the extra pensions. The existence of an earnings-related component in a pension scheme therefore has a positive incentive effect and raises average earnings in comparison with a flat-rate pension.

The chapter also examined the maximisation of a social welfare function specified in terms of individuals' utility levels, and considered the trade-off between average utility and its inequality. It was found that the trade-off displays a backward-bending section whereby, above a certain tax rate, further increases in the tax rate both reduce average utility and increase inequality. This was particularly pronounced for the logarithmic cardinalisation of the utility function.

A major result is that, in terms of the trade-off between equity and efficiency implied by the social welfare function adopted, the flat-rate pension dominates the two-tier pension. A higher social indifference curve can always be reached using a flat-rate pension. Although analytical results cannot be obtained, this result was found to be robust in the face of variations in parameter values.

Chapter 9

Pensions and Compensating Variations

This chapter examines the compensating variations in wages arising from the existence of pension schemes. It has long been recognised that comparisons of earnings in different firms or occupations should recognise the existence of pension schemes because they provide a form of deferred pay. It is also important to distinguish between compensating variations for individuals and equalising differences in the market. The latter only reflect compensating variations at the margin, where a decision regarding labour mobility is relevant. Empirical studies therefore typically concentrate on the measurement of such equalising differences. For discussions of the theory, see Smith (1979), Brown (1980) and Rosen (1986).

The purpose of this chapter is to examine the nature of the trade-off between wages and pensions from the point of view of an individual worker, using a simple utility maximising model. The approach used is to consider combinations of wage rates and pensions between which a worker is indifferent. While the empirical literature has looked for a negative (unitary) coefficient on pension costs in logarithmic regressions, it is not obvious that basic theory would predict such a relationship within a utility maximising framework.

Comparisons are made for flat-rate pension schemes and two-tier schemes in which a basic pension is augmented by an earnings-related component equal to some proportion of earnings measured above the basic pension. The comparisons are made in the context of a two-period model whereby the worker makes a labour supply decision relating to work in the first period, and retires in the second period. The pension may of course be augmented by private savings. Allowance for labour supply responses makes it possible also to consider earnings, as well as wage rates, and pension combinations which give the same utility to the worker. The results obtained using this simple framework suggest that the relevant elasticities are unlikely to be constant and may take a wide range of values depending on tastes, wage levels and the type of pension formula. In some cases they may indeed be positive.

First, section 9.1 discusses earlier literature. Section 9.2 presents the two-period framework of analysis, for both flat-rate and earnings-related pension schemes. It is found that unequivocal results cannot be obtained for general utility and tax functions, so it is necessary to add some more structure to the model. Results for a Cobb-Douglas form of utility function and a linear income tax are then given in section 9.3. An alternative approach is briefly considered in section 9.4.

9.1   Previous Literature

Attempts to measure wage-pension trade-offs have, however, achieved only limited success. Studies from the early 1980s include Ehrenberg (1980), Schiller and Weiss (1980) and Smith (1981) and used a variety of data sets and approaches. The common feature of these studies was that in regressions of the logarithm of wages on a set of variables, including the logarithm of pension costs, the hypothesis to be tested from the basic theory was that the constant elasticity of wages with respect to the pension should be minus unity. There was little support for this hypothesis and in some cases the coefficient was found to have the 'wrong' sign. This failure to obtain empirical support for the theory of compensating variations was initially attributed to the use of inappropriate data and the wrong estimation method (namely ordinary least squares).

In a detailed discussion of the problem of estimating such trade-offs, Smith and Ehrenberg (1983) stressed the need for employer-based data on pension costs in order to estimate the annual increment in the present value of pension benefits, for comparison with the annual wage. They also suggested that in many schemes the pension is itself a function of wages and other pension characteristics, so that when this 'technical' relationship is modelled a two-stage-least-squares estimation procedure should be used. The third requirement stressed by Smith and Ehrenberg was that the variables reflecting the other factors which influence wages (such as education and age) are not usually found in employer-based data sets, so that employer and employee (household) data sets need to be combined. Using a special set of data which satisfied these requirements, they nevertheless found no evidence of a significant trade-off. In discussing their disappointing results, Smith and Ehrenberg suggested that a major problem arises from omitted variables bias associated with unobserved worker characteristics. Subsequently, Hwong *et al.* (1992) have shown more formally that unobserved productivity can indeed lead to a substantial bias in the estimation of compensating wage differentials, though their analysis does not include pensions.

More recently Gunderson *et al.* (1992) examined wage-pension trade-offs in collective agreements involving flat-benefit pension plans. They followed the advice of Smith and Ehrenberg (1983) and used a data set obtained by merging pension and collective agreement data. They also provide a useful tubular survey of other empirical studies (1992, p.148). Gunderson *et al.* were able to find stronger support for the idea of a trade-off, but it was nevertheless not as strong as expected.

A common feature of all the studies mentioned above is that they use an annual measure of earnings as the dependent variable, thereby ignoring the age-earnings profile. However, Smith and Ehrenberg (1983) used a dichotomous variable indicating the existence of mandatory retirement; this was intended to capture the idea, following Lazear (1979), that such firms would have relatively steeper earnings profiles. The studies also typically ignore the tax system applying either to pension or earnings. Furthermore, possible labour supply effects are also ignored. The existence of a pension may be expected to have implications for labour supply and the precise effect will depend on the structure of the pension plan. The preferences of workers, including those for leisure and consumption as well as their time preference rates, are therefore relevant. In view of these many complications, it is by no means clear that the assumption of a unit elasticity is appropriate.

9.2   The Basic Model

This section presents the analysis of the wage-pension trade-off for a single individual maximising a lifetime utility function, and allowing for income taxation during the working life. Allowing for labour supply decisions means that a distinction can be drawn between the wage rate and the level of earnings. Flat-rate and earnings-related schemes are examined separately.

9.2.1   A Flat-rate Pension

As in earlier chapters, divide the individual's life into two periods of 'work' and 'retirement'. Consumption in each period is c_1 and c_2 respectively. Let the proportion of total time available in the working period which is devoted to leisure be denoted $h < 1$. The interest rate is r, with $v = 1/(1+r)$. Furthermore, the individual's wage rate, earnings and tax paid in the first period are respectively w, y and $T(y)$. Consider the maximisation of utility, $U(c_1, c_2, h)$, subject to the following lifetime budget constraint:

$$c_1 + vc_2 = y + vp - T(y) \tag{9.1}$$

where p is the flat-rate (untaxed) pension received in retirement, and gross earnings, y, are given by:

$$y = w(1 - h) \tag{9.2}$$

This formulation abstracts from interest-income taxation, but it may easily be modified, as discussed below. After specifying a form for the utility function and the tax function, this optimisation problem can be solved to give, after substituting the optimal values in the direct utility function, the indirect utility function $V = V(w, p)$. In this type of problem, care needs to be taken with corner solutions, particularly as the tax function is usually non-linear.

The indirect utility function can then be used to consider variations in w and p for which the individual is indifferent. Thus, total differentiation gives:

$$\frac{dw}{dp} = -\frac{\partial V/\partial p}{\partial V/\partial w} \tag{9.3}$$

If it is required to consider a change from a zero value to some positive value of p, or to examine other discrete changes, from p to say p', then of course (9.3) can no longer be used and it is necessary to solve the equation $V(w,p) = V(w',p')$ for the new wage rate, w', which gives the same utility. For some forms of the utility function, explicit solutions for w' may not be available, so that numerical methods are required. The following analysis concentrates on small changes, assuming that interior solutions to the individual's optimisation problem apply.

A convenient way to express the compensating variation is to define the elasticity of the wage rate with respect to the pension, η_w, so that:

$$\eta_w = \frac{p}{w}\frac{dw}{dp} \tag{9.4}$$

This elasticity will be negative, but in general the value of η_w will be expected to depend on the wage rate as well as the preferences of the individual. However, as discussed above, empirical studies have examined earnings rather than wage rates. Hence, define the elasticity of earnings with respect to the pension, η_y, as:

$$\eta_y = \frac{p}{y}\frac{dy}{dp} \tag{9.5}$$

The relationship between η_y and η_w is given, using (9.2) and (9.4) by:

$$\eta_y = \eta_w \left\{ 1 + \frac{w}{1-h}\frac{d(1-h)}{dw} \right\} \tag{9.6}$$

The second term in the curly brackets in (9.6) is the wage elasticity of the supply of labour, denoted η_L. If this elasticity is positive and leisure is a 'normal' good, the compensating variation in terms of earnings, η_y, exceeds (in absolute terms), the value of η_L. If $\eta_L = -1$, $\eta_y = 0$ whatever the value of η_w, although such a 'backward-bending' supply curve is obviously unlikely. The concentration on earnings rather than wage rates may therefore give a misleading indication of the existence or otherwise of compensating variations. Furthermore, it would not be appropriate simply to standardise for hours worked because of the endogeneity of hours and their dependence on the pension itself. There is certainly no *a priori* reason why the elasticity η_y should be minus unity.

It might perhaps be suggested that the compensating variation should be measured in terms of the extent to which the wage rate, or the value of earnings, changes in response to an increase in pension contributions by an employer, rather than a change in the pension itself. Indeed, the empirical literature uses pension costs as the independent variable in regression analyses. However, it can easily be seen that the two approaches yield identical results. For example, an employer's contribution of e, during the working period, to a private pension scheme yields a pension of $p = e(1 + i)$, where i is the after-tax rate of return achieved by the private scheme and will typically exceed the after-tax market rate of interest at which individuals lend. Hence the proportional increase in p is identical to the proportional increase in e. The same is true of the earnings-related pension scheme discussed in the next sub-section.

9.2.2   An Earnings-related Pension

Suppose that, in addition to a flat-rate component of the pension, there is an earnings-related pension. The individual's budget constraint is thus the same as (9.1), but with p defined as:

$$p = a + s(y - a) \tag{9.7}$$

where the term a is the flat-rate component and s is the earnings-related proportion. The expression in (9.7) only applies for $y > a$, so that in solving the optimisation problem, further care needs to be taken with corner solutions, in addition to those generated by the form of $T(y)$. The question of interest at this point is how the wage rate and earnings must change in response to an increase in the earnings-related proportion, s, in order to keep utility constant. Hence the indirect utility function can be written as $V = V(w, s)$. The pension, p, is now endogenous as in (9.7) and the elasticity, η_w, must be re-defined as:

$$\eta_w = \frac{pdw}{wds}\frac{ds}{dp} \tag{9.8}$$

It is again clear that η_w will be negative, but the corresponding value of η_y is not so straightforward. Although equation (9.6) is still appropriate, it is necessary to recognise the complication arising from the endogeneity of the pension. This implies that:

$$\frac{dh}{dw} = \frac{dh}{ds}\left(\frac{dp}{ds}\right)^{-1}\left(\frac{dw}{dp}\right)^{-1} \tag{9.9}$$

where:

$$\frac{dw}{dp} = \frac{dw}{ds}\frac{ds}{dp} = -\frac{\partial V/\partial s}{\partial V/\partial w}\frac{ds}{dp} \tag{9.10}$$

$$\frac{dp}{ds} = \frac{dw}{ds}\frac{\partial p}{\partial w} + \frac{\partial p}{\partial s} \tag{9.11}$$

$$\frac{dh}{ds} = \frac{dw}{ds}\frac{\partial h}{\partial w} + \frac{\partial h}{\partial s} \tag{9.12}$$

Consider the signs of the above terms. The term dw/ds is, as already established, negative. The partial derivatives $\partial p/\partial w$ and $\partial p/\partial s$ will be positive, so the sign of dp/ds in (9.11) is not obvious *a priori*. Hence the sign of dw/dp in (9.10) is also uncertain. Similarly, the sign of (9.12) cannot be established on *a priori* grounds without adding more structure to the model. However, unlike the case of a flat-rate pension, there is now a stronger probability that dh/dw is positive, so that not only may $|\eta_y|$ be less than $|\eta_w|$, but η_y may actually be positive. Examples of positive η_y are reported in the next section. In the empirical work mentioned above, a positive value has nevertheless been taken as evidence rejecting the theory of compensating variations.

9.3   Specific Functional Forms

It has been seen that, in general, the sign of the elasticity η_y cannot be obtained *a priori*, particularly in the case where there is an earnings-related component to the pension scheme. This section therefore explores the model further by specifying a particular tax function and utility function. The simplest approach is to suppose that there is a linear income tax, so that:

$$T(y) = ty - a \tag{9.13}$$

and those with $ty < a$ effectively pay a negative amount of tax. For convenience, it is assumed that the unconditional transfer, a, is the same as the flat-rate pension component of the earnings-related scheme. The easiest form of utility function to use is one in which utility in each period is the logarithmic form of a simple Cobb-Douglas utility function, with a time-preference rate of $(1 - \theta)/\theta$. Hence U can be written:

$$U = \alpha \log c_1 + (1 - \alpha) \log h + \theta \alpha \log c_2 \tag{9.14}$$

This form of utility function is of course just a three-good Cobb-Douglas utility function, so the solution to the optimisation problem is quite straightforward. This requires the specification of 'full income', M, which is the maximum (present value of) net income which the individual could obtain; that is, net income when $h = 0$. The general form of interior solutions for the Cobb-Douglas utility function is that the consumption of each good is a fixed proportion of the ratio of M to the price of that good, with the proportion being the exponent on the particular good divided by the sum of the exponents on all goods. In this case the price of consumption in each period is unity and the price of leisure is the net wage $w(1 - t)$. Hence, for example, leisure is given immediately as:

$$h = \frac{(1 - \alpha) M}{(1 + \alpha\theta) w (1 - t)} \tag{9.15}$$

This result holds only for w above the threshold wage rate for which $h < 1$. The two alternative budget constraints which imply different forms of M are examined in the following subsections.

9.3.1 A Flat-rate Pension

With a flat-rate pension of p, write the individuals 'full income', M, as:

$$M = a + vp + w(1 - t) \qquad (9.16)$$

where M is equal to the present value of net income which would be received when $h = 0$. The interior solutions for h, c_1 and c_2 can be obtained using the general result for the Cobb-Douglas form described above. Substituting the resulting expressions into the utility function in (9.14) and rearranging gives the indirect utility function as follows:

$$V = K + (1 + \alpha\theta) \log M - (1 - \alpha) \log \{w(1 - t)\} \qquad (9.17)$$

where K is a constant. Thus, appropriate differentiation and substitution into (9.3) and (9.4) gives:

$$\eta_w = \frac{-vp(1 + \alpha\theta)}{\alpha(1 + \theta)w(1 - t) - (1 - \alpha)(vp + a)} \qquad (9.18)$$

and from (9.15), $dh/dw < 0$, so that $|\eta_y| > |\eta_w|$. Suppose, for example, that $r = 0.2$, $a = 1$, $t = 0.3$, $p = 1.5$ and $\theta = 0.8$ (the time preference rate is 0.25). When $a = 0.7$ it can be found for a wage rate of $w = 2$ that η_w and η_y are -1.79 and -2.90 respectively, but are -0.683 and -0.845 when $w = 4$. For a lower value of $a = 0.65$, the elasticities are -2.23 and -4.30 respectively when $w = 2$, and -0.76 and -1.01 for $w = 4$.

It can be seen from (9.18) that a reduction in the rate of interest, implying an increase in v, leads to an increase in the absolute value of the wage elasticity. If there is an interest income tax, then allowance must be made for a further kink in the budget constraint, imposing the after-tax interest rate of $r(1 - t)$ over the range where the individual lends. This is slightly more cumbersome, but it can be found, not surprisingly given the effect of a reduction in the interest rate, that over the relevant range the absolute values of η_w and η_y are higher than for the cases considered in the previous paragraph.

9.3.2   An Earnings-related Pension

The earnings-related pension in (9.7) can be combined with the specifications of the tax and utility functions in (9.13) and (9.14). It can be seen in this case that full income, M, becomes:

$$M = a\{1 + v(1 - s)\} + w(1 - t + sv) \tag{9.19}$$

The implication of the earnings-related pension component is that effective rates of income tax falls from t to $t - sv$. The indirect utility function is therefore obtained as a straightforward modification of (9.17), giving:

$$V = K' + (1 + aq)\log M - (1 - a)\log\{w(1 - t + sv)\} \tag{9.20}$$

where K' is a constant and M is given by (9.19). The examination of the various terms in equations (9.8) to (9.12) is rather tedious, but is otherwise straightforward and is therefore not reproduced here. The major results are as follows. The existence of the earnings-related component can be seen to provide a labour supply incentive, so that $dh/ds < 0$. The resulting higher earnings imply that $dp/ds > 0$ and, with $dw/dp < 0$, the term dh/dw is positive, unlike the flat-rate pension case. This means that the fall in labour supply resulting from the compensating reduction in the wage rate is outweighed by the increase in labour supply resulting from the increase in the proportional pension rate. The net result is that both the pension and gross earnings are higher.

For all the cases given earlier, but with $s = 0.1$ and p determined endogenously, it is found that $|\eta_y| > |\eta_w|$. For the low wage of $w = 2$, the values of η_y are in fact positive (and are greater than 2), although they remain negative for the higher wage of $w = 4$. Empirical estimates which find higher earnings associated with higher pensions do not therefore necessarily contradict the suggestion that there are compensating wage rate variations. The sensitivity of the results to the basic assumptions regarding the wage and taste parameters also suggests the possibility of substantial intra-marginal rents.

9.4 Alternative Comparisons

The above discussion has concentrated on finding combinations of pensions and wage rates (or earnings) between which an individual is indifferent. An individual is considered to compare alternative 'packages' of wage and pension combinations and make a decision about which job to accept. Consider an alternative type of comparison in which the individual has the opportunity to invest a proportion of earnings into a company-operated pension scheme. The elasticity, η_w, therefore needs to be reinterpreted; it now measures the ratio of the proportional reduction in the wage rate to the proportional increase in the pension, where the latter is financed by the employee's own contributions to a pension scheme. The elasticity will obviously be very much lower than in the previous section.

If the net-of-tax rate of return offered by the company scheme is the same as the net rate of return obtained in the market, and contributions are not exempt from income taxation, it is obvious that the company scheme is irrelevant; there is no reason why an individual would accept a lower wage rate since the timing of receipts does not affect lifetime wealth. Suppose, however, that the company pension offers a net rate of return of i, and that a proportion, q, of earnings can be invested in the scheme. Suppose also that such contributions are tax-deductible, so that income taxation is based on earnings net of contributions. The budget constraint is therefore:

$$c_1 + vc_2 = a + w(1-h)(1-q)(1-t) + vp \qquad (9.21)$$

where the (untaxed) pension, p, is given by:

$$p = qw(1-h)(1+i) \qquad (9.22)$$

Substitution of (9.22) into (9.21) and rearranging gives:

$$c_1 + vc_2 = a + w(1-h)\left[1 - t + q\left\{v(1+i) - (1-t)\right\}\right] \qquad (9.23)$$

The new budget constraint (9.23) shows that the effect of the scheme is to reduce the effective income tax rate facing the individual. Even if

$i = r$, the opportunity with tax deductibility to shift earnings into a later period, when the returns in the form of the pension do not attract taxation, is advantageous. The individual would be prepared to accept a lower wage rate in return for the opportunity to carry out such inter-temporal adjustments more favourably than elsewhere. It would of course be necessary to impose a restriction on the value of q in order to ensure that the effective tax rate does not fall below some minimum, say t_m. Hence, the following constraint would be imposed:

$$q < \frac{t - t_m}{v(1 + i) - 1 + t} \tag{9.24}$$

The appropriate comparison is therefore as follows. An increase in q leads, via equation (9.22), to an increase in the pension, p, even allowing for the reduction in w (and consequently also $1 - h$) that would leave lifetime utility unchanged. The elasticity η_w is the resulting proportionate reduction in w divided by the proportionate rise in p. It is not surprising that the elasticities are much lower than earlier. The present framework has excluded other sources of income in the second or retirement period, so that the individual necessarily lends in the first period; this implies that an increase in q, *ceteris paribus*, would necessarily increase utility.

9.5   Conclusions

This chapter examined compensating wage differentials for an individual worker in a two-period framework in which labour supply is endogenous. Comparisons were made for a flat-rate pension and a two-tier scheme, and allowance was made for the existence of taxes and other transfer payments. The results generate quite different elasticities according to assumptions made regarding tastes of the individual, and particularly the wage rate. In addition, the elasticities of earnings with respect to pensions can take both positive and negative values. The empirical literature has ignored labour supply effects and has concentrated on double-log regressions of earnings on pension costs and other characteristics of workers and firms, and has been looking for a coefficient on the logarithm of pension costs of minus unity. The failure to obtain this result was first explained in terms of the data and estimation method used, and was then later attributed to the bias arising from unobserved individual characteristics.

This chapter argued instead that the basic specification used in empirical studies is inappropriate, along with the *a priori* expectation that the existence of compensating wage differentials implies a (negative) unit elasticity. Using a utility maximising lifetime model, it has been shown that the appropriate elasticities are very sensitive to assumptions regarding preferences, and particularly the level of wage rates. A model of individuals' behaviour was examined explicitly, paying careful attention to the tax structure as well as the pension structure, along with the endogeneity of labour supply. The results suggest a degree of pessimism regarding the ability to measure empirically the extent of such variations using standard regression techniques.

Part IV

Lifetime Simulations

Chapter 10

Alternative Pension Systems

Previous parts of this book have examined population ageing and a variety of pension models. This part turns to a more detailed examination of specific pension arrangements. Substantial use is made of lifetime simulations, which are necessary given the complexity of pension schemes and the difficulty of deriving analytical results in a lifetime framework. The simulations focus on the lifetime experience of a single cohort of individuals, so inter-generational comparisons cannot be made.

Many nations are considering a range of options to reduce the long term financial burden of providing previously promised levels of state pensions; see World Bank (1994). Tactics suggested to reduce the emerging difficulties include: an increased degree of means-testing in respect of state pensions; a shift from an unfunded public provision to a funded mandatory system administered and invested in the private sector; higher retirement ages; increased contributions by employers and employees; and reductions in the level of taxation support for pension schemes.

In view of these developments it is useful to consider the existing Australian arrangements where the government pension, known as the age pension, is fully means-tested (there is no universal component), there is a mandatory superannuation system funded and administered in the private sector and there is taxation on pension fund contributions, fund investment income and benefits. Some lessons may emerge as a result of focusing on the Australian system as it contains some of the features being considered by other countries.

The purpose of this chapter is to evaluate the redistributive implications of the current system in Australia in terms of the lifetime incomes of members of a single cohort and to compare this system with two alternative schemes. The alternatives incorporate a universal pension and other features which are closer to the arrangements in many other countries. Attention is restricted to the experience of a cohort of males in continuous employment. Each individual is also assumed to be a homeowner: this is used for the purpose of administering the Australian means-tests.

In section 10.1 retirement income programmes are discussed and the unique Australian arrangements are contrasted with those found in many OECD countries. Further details of the Australian system are then described in section 10.2. The two alternative structures are presented in section 10.3. The basic simulation model is described briefly in section 10.4, and the three schemes are compared in section 10.5.

10.1   Retirement Income Programmes

10.1.1   International Context and Developments

Programmes to provide retirement income vary widely around the world. Some are dominated by a centrally managed scheme whereas others have very little government involvement and are concentrated in the private sector, under either employer or individual control. In many nations, informal arrangements are more dominant than formal schemes. The Australian arrangements are unique among OECD nations and it is therefore necessary to place these arrangements within the context of other national retirement income schemes.

The World Bank report (1994) suggested that there are three 'pillars' in the provision of retirement income. These are the public pension pillar managed by the government, the occupational pension pillar managed within the private sector and the voluntary personal savings pillar. The relative importance of each pillar varies widely.

Many European and North American countries have a government pension system based on a pay-as-you-go funding basis, with each year's contributions (from both employers and workers) paying for the pensions provided in that year. In many cases, the total pension paid is a combination of a flat-rate pension and an additional pension linked to a measure of the individual's lifetime earnings or contributions. There may also be a means-tested supplementary pension available, perhaps as part of the welfare system.

The relative importance of the government pension system determines the significance of the occupational pension system managed within the private sector. Where the public system provides generous benefits, for example, in Italy or Spain, a less significant occupational pension arrangement operates. By contrast, if the level of the public pension is smaller or permits contracting-out, as in Canada and the UK respectively, the occupational pension schemes are more important; on UK and European systems, see Blake (1992) and Dilnot *et al.* (1994).

Many governments are being forced to reconsider their unfunded public sector pension plans. Typically, actions that have been taken to reduce costs include the introduction of means-tests for part of the pension, as in New Zealand, the reduction in the amount of the pension, such as in the UK for the earnings-related component, and the raising of the entitlement age, as in the US.

Within this context of change, the Australian system can be seen to incorporate some of the changes under consideration. It is therefore instructive to assess some of the consequences of a system like the Australian one so that countries which are considering incorporating features of this system into their own arrangements (such as the introduction of means-testing) are better placed to make an informed decision.

10.1.2 Unique Australian Characteristics

The Australian system contrasts with those found in many countries. There is no public pension programme associated with employment. A means-tested age pension, funded by general taxation revenue and not by specific contributions, is payable to an individual who has income and assets below certain prescribed limits. Currently about 53 per cent of the aged population receive the full pension (which is equivalent to approximately 26 per cent of the average wage) while another 27 per cent receive a reduced pension. The remaining 20 per cent of the aged population receive no pension from the government since their assets or their level of income from employment, business, or investment, exceeds the prescribed limits.

The provision of retirement benefits in the private sector is compulsory. Currently, employers must contribute 5 per cent or 6 per cent of earnings to a regulated pension (that is, superannuation) fund. This minimum contribution rate is planned to rise to 9 per cent of earnings in 2002 and to be further supported by a mandatory minimum employee contribution of 3 per cent of earnings from 1999. These funds are subject to solvency requirements (they must be fully funded), are administered in the private sector (either through corporate, industry or personal plans) and are permitted to invest in areas that are consistent with the investment objectives set by the individual fund's trustees, with relatively few restrictions.

A reason for the government's introduction of mandatory contributions is that the development of a comprehensive superannuation system will reduce the future cost of the means-tested age pension due to the availability of funded superannuation benefits. It is argued that a total contribution rate of 12 per cent of earnings is sufficient for many employees to provide an adequate level of retirement income; see Dawkins (1992).

Hence, in terms of the three tiers of retirement income mentioned above, the Australian situation can be summarised as follows:

(i) the public pillar is restricted to a means-tested age pension financed from general taxation and thus there is no universal base pension;

(ii) the occupational pillar is provided by the minimum contributions by employers and employees on a fully funded basis, and is administered by and invested in the private sector;

(iii) the voluntary savings pillar is provided by additional contributions by employers and/or individuals within, or outside, the superannuation system.

Integration of the first two pillars, namely the means-tested age pension and occupational retirement benefits, is incomplete. Some commentators have suggested that the abolition of the means-test would improve this integration and clarify the incentives within the total system; see World Bank (1994) and Institute of Actuaries of Australia (1994). This chapter evaluates the redistributive implication of the abolition of the means-tests. Although this research arises from an Australian context, many national retirement programmes are considering the introduction of a degree of means-testing into their schemes; hence, the results should be of interest to those countries.

Another fundamental difference between the Australian arrangements and those in place in many developed economies is the method of taxation of pensions. In most OECD countries, contributions made to pension plans by employers and employees are in many cases tax-deductible and are not subject to any tax when received by the pension fund. Furthermore, the investment income earned by the pension fund is exempt from taxation. However, the benefits paid from the fund in the form of pensions are normally subject to taxation at income tax rates, and benefits taken as a lump sum are taxed at special rates. This pattern of taxation is sometimes known as the EET (Exempt/Exempt/Tax) system, since taxation is deferred until benefits are received; see Knox (1990) and Dilnot and Johnson (1993).

The Australian system in its mature form is described briefly in Table 10.1. This uses terms that are unique to the Australian system. 'Undeducted contributions' are the sum of employee contributions which have not been taken as a deduction against income tax. The remainder of the benefit is called the 'taxable benefit' and includes all interest earned by both the undeducted and tax-deductible contributions. The 'excessive' proportion of a lump sum is that proportion in excess of a maximum 'reasonable benefit' level of $400,000. If less than 50 per cent of the superannuation fund is taken as a lump sum, the maximum reasonable benefit level is $800,000. The 'undeducted purchase price' (UPP) for a superannuation annuity is that part of

Table 10.1: The Tax Structure in Australia

Contribution rates	Employer 9%, Employee 3%
Contribution tax	15% on tax deductible Employer contributions
Employee Contribution rebate	10% of employee contributions, subject to tests on income (maximum rebate $100, maximum salary $31,000) and age related maxima on total contributions. Rebate may not exeed tax liability.
Superannuation Fund Earnings	Nominal rate of tax of 15%, assumed to be an effective rate of 7.5%, allowing for credits.
Lump Sum Tax	Undeducted contributions not subject to lump sum tax. The taxable benefit included in lump sum is subject to 16.4% tax on amounts in excess of a threshold ($77,796 in 1993-94). Excessive amounts taxed at 48.4%. Rates include the Medicare levy.
Age Pension	Taxable age pension payable subject to income and asset means-tests. Income tax rebate depending on income.
Annuities in payment	Superannuation annuity taxed as income, except that UPP is exempt.
	Other annuities taxed as income, except the purchase price allowance which is exempt.
Superannuation pension rebate	15% rebate associated with contribution tax.

the cost of the annuity attributed to undeducted contributions, divided by the expected term of payment.

In Australia, all tax-deductible contributions received by a fund are subject to a flat 15 per cent contributions tax, paid on receipt by the fund. In addition, investment income is taxed at the 15 per cent rate, although various investment credits reduce the effective rate to between 5 per cent and 10 per cent. Benefits are also subject to tax, although the tax rates have been reduced to compensate for the 15 per cent tax on contributions. In essence, taxation is paid on Australian pension funds at every stage: when contributions are made, as they accumulate and finally, when benefits are received. There is no doubt that these arrangements are complex. The next section describes the system in more detail.

10.2 The Australian System

10.2.1 Superannuation Taxation Before Retirement

The long-term government objective for superannuation contributions is an employer contribution of 9 per cent of earnings and employee contributions of 3 per cent of earnings. Although the 1995-6 Federal Budget announced a proposal for the government to match dollar for dollar employee contributions (subject to certain maximum and income limits), this chapter ignores this government contribution as there is some doubt as to its future introduction.

The current system is modelled in the following way. Define X as the level of the individual's gross annual earnings. Employer contributions are $0.09X$, and employee contributions are $0.03X$. Let T_c represent the tax on deductible employer contributions; then $T_c = 0.15 \times 0.09X = 0.0135X$. The net contribution to superannuation each year is therefore equal to $0.1065X$

Assuming that these contributions are made on average in mid-year, that the superannuation fund (SF_t at time t) earns rate i per year, and that there is a net tax on investment earnings (after allowing for imputation and other credits) of 7.5 per cent, and I represents the net investment income received in the year, then:

$$SF_t = SF_t - 1 + 0.925I + 0.1065X \tag{10.1}$$

where $I = i(SF_{t-1} + 0.5 \times 0.1065X)$.

An employee may be entitled to a tax rebate in respect of undeducted employee contributions. However, the level of the rebate is limited to 10 per cent of the employee's contributions subject to a maximum of $100 per annum. It is also income-tested so that any individual with earnings in excess of $31,000 receives no rebate. There is also a restriction linked to age and the level of the employer's contribution but this rarely applies due to the severity of the income testing. There is also a tax rebate payable to low-income earners. Let R represent the total rebates payable.

Assuming that there are no other sources of income, income tax, T_X, is calculated on the value of gross earnings, X, rounded down to the nearest dollar. The Medicare levy (in respect of compulsory medical insurance) is also added. The total income tax payable by the individual, T, since rebates may not exceed the amount of tax assessed, may be written as:

$$T = \text{Max}\,[T_X + \text{Medicare levy} - R, 0] \qquad (10.2)$$

The individual's disposable income, A, is defined as the gross earnings less employee superannuation contributions less income tax payable, so that $A = 0.97X - T$.

In addition, non-superannuation savings may be accumulated each year in a fund (of F_t after t years). Assume that savings are made on average in mid-year, that the gross annual nominal rate of interest earned on savings is r, and that the effective tax rate on interest income is 25 per cent. This flat rate has been chosen as it is not appropriate to assume that interest income is simply added to income from employment for income tax purposes, due to the wide range of investment opportunities available. Hence, if S is the amount of non-superannuation savings made in the year, the value of F_t at the end of year t is:

$$F_t = F_{t-1} + 0.75r(F_{t-1} + 0.5S) + S \qquad (10.3)$$

10.2.2   Taxation in Retirement

Taxation in retirement includes a number of components including a tax on any lump sum benefit, tax on any superannuation pension or annuity and other income tax. The lump sum tax, T_L, is calculated as follows, with a threshold of \$77,796 (as applied in the 1993-94 tax year). First, if there is no 'excessive benefit', define L_T as the taxable post-1983 lump sum benefit excluding undeducted contributions. Then, if $L_T \leq 77,796$ then $T_L = 0$, but if $L_T > 77,796$, then $T_L = 0.164(L_T - 77,796)$.

The taxable benefit is considered excessive when it exceeds \$400,000 (if more than half the fund is taken as a lump sum) or \$800,000 in other circumstances. If there is an excessive benefit, then:

$$T_L = 0.164\{L_T(1 - E) - 77,796\} + 0.484L_T E \qquad (10.4)$$

where E is the proportion of the superannuation benefit (excluding the amount of undeducted contributions) that qualifies as 'excessive'.

Part of the income arising from purchased annuities is subject to normal personal income taxation and the Medicare levy. The taxable component for annuities purchased by after-tax capital (either savings or from after-tax lump sum benefits) is the annual income, less the purchase price divided by 14.6. The deduction represents a spreading of the capital cost over the expected term of the annuity, in this case, a life expectancy of 14.6 years for a male aged 65. For non-excessive superannuation annuities, the taxable portion is the annual income, less the amount of undeducted contributions divided by 14.6.

Finally, there exists a special income tax rebate relating to superannuation annuities which is designed to allow for the 15 per cent contributions tax levied during the accumulation period of the fund. This rebate is 15 per cent of the non-excessive proportion of the taxable annuity purchased by the superannuation taxable benefit.

10.2.3 Eligibility for the Age Pension

The amount of age pension awarded is subject to independent means-tests of income and assets, which depend on the marital status of the pensioner and whether or not the pensioner is a homeowner. Non-homeowners are permitted to hold a higher value of assets than homeowners before the means-test disqualifies them from eligibility. The individuals considered in this study are assumed to be homeowners. The full rate of pension for single individuals in 1994 was \$8,115 per annum.

The full rate of pension may be reduced depending on the income of the retiree. The income which is subject to the means-test includes all taxable income from sources other than the age pension, but excludes the repayment of capital amounts in any annuity. If Y is the level of income subject to the income test, the reduction in the age pension, R_P, is:

$$
\begin{aligned}
R_p &= 0 && \text{for } Y \leq 2,236 \\
&= 0.5Y - 2,236 && \text{for } 2,236 \leq Y \leq 18,466 \\
&= 8,115 && \text{for } Y > 18,466
\end{aligned}
\tag{10.5}
$$

The pension payable also depends on the asset test limitations. In the cases considered in this study, a retiree has only three relevant assets. These are:

(i) an interest-bearing bank account, in which case the balance in the account is an assessable asset. It is also assumed that the bank balance is reduced by capital drawings each year in such a way as to extinguish the account at age 80;

(ii) an annuity purchased using after-tax money, when the entitlement to the remaining future income stream is deemed to have an assessable asset value. If N is the number of complete years since the first annuity payment, the asset value of the assessable future whole life income stream is taken to be purchase price multiplied by $(14.6 - N)/14.6$. Hence, this component of the asset test ceases to have any relevance beyond age 80;

(iii) an annuity purchased directly by a superannuation benefit which is not assessable under the assets test.

Where applicable, the reduction in the pension arising from the asset test, R_a, is given by:

$$
\begin{aligned}
R_a &= 0 && \text{for assets} \leq 112,750 \\
&= 0.078(\text{assets} - 112,750) && \text{for } 112,750 \leq \text{assets} \leq 216,788 \\
&= 8,115 && \text{for assets} \geq 216,788
\end{aligned}
\tag{10.6}
$$

The threshold value of \$112,750 is that which applies to homeowners who are single. The actual age pension paid is the lesser one resulting from the independent application of the income test and the assets test.

A tax rebate, P_r, may also be received by some age pensioners. Where Y_t represents taxable income, this is calculated as:

$$
\begin{aligned}
P_r &= 972 & \text{for } Y_t \leq \$10,260 \\
&= 972 - 0.125(Y_t - 10,260) & \text{for } 10,260 \leq Y_t \leq 18,036 \\
&= 0 & \text{for } Y_t > 18,036 \qquad (10.7)
\end{aligned}
$$

If a pension rebate is payable, the tax payer is also exempt from the Medicare levy.

10.2.4 Retirement Decisions

At retirement, the individual transforms assets accumulated during working life, from superannuation and non-superannuation savings, into immediate expenditure, interest-bearing assets and annuities. The superannuation benefit is divided into two components according to their source; namely the employee's 'undeducted contributions' and the balance of the fund, called the 'taxable benefit'. This includes all employer contributions and all investment income earned by the fund, including that earned by the undeducted contributions. These two components are treated differently for taxation purposes, as are the lump sums or annuities arising from them. Where only part of the superannuation benefit is taken as a lump sum, the two components are split in the same proportion between the lump sum and any annuity purchase.

Many options are available in choosing how to receive the superannuation benefit, each having different tax and age pension implications. For example, all the superannuation benefit may be taken as a lump sum benefit, the appropriate level of lump sum tax paid, and the after-tax benefit may be combined with other savings before considering the purchase of an annuity. Once the lump sum tax has been paid on a superannuation benefit, the resulting capital is no longer identified in terms of its source. In contrast, if the superannuation benefit is used to purchase an annuity directly without incurring a liability to lump sum tax, the annuity continues to be identified as arising from the superannuation benefit for the purposes of income taxation and the age pension means-tests. Hence, the source of the capital used to purchase annuity income has continuing implications for taxation and age pension entitlement.

10.3   Alternative Reforms

The current Australian scheme makes it very difficult for individuals and policy makers to make appropriate plans, and introduces a number of disincentives; see Atkinson *et al.* (1995). The means-testing of the age pension provides a disincentive to save or accept employment over a wide range of incomes, and a strong incentive to take the superannuation benefit as a lump sum and to spend some of this at retirement. This is demonstrated by the bunching of the income distribution of retired individuals at the lower threshold of the means-test; see Creedy and Disney (1990).

Recognition of these problems led the Institute of Actuaries of Australia (1994) to propose a revision of the Australian retirement income policy. The proposed structure incorporated a universal, taxable age pension and a simplified taxation system for superannuation. These features are key elements in the two alternatives presented here.

The major problems with the Australian system are the complex taxation arrangements for superannuation and the lack of integration between the superannuation and age pension systems. The lack of integration is reflected in: differences in entitlement ages, with the superannuation preservation age being 55 and the pension ages being 65 or 60; differences in the form which benefits take since the major proportion of superannuation benefits is paid as lump sums while the means-tested pension is provided in income form; conflicting incentive effects, with the existence of the means-tests discouraging additional savings and post-retirement investment while the taxation incentives for superannuation exist to encourage savings; and differing bases for calculating the benefit entitlements as superannuation benefits broadly reflect the total level of lifetime earnings while the age pension is a fixed amount, independent of the individual's past earnings levels.

The two alternative structures examined in this chapter address these defects in the current system. The integration problems can be overcome with the provision of a universal taxable age pension and a corresponding reduction in the level of compulsory superannuation contributions. The abolition of the means-tests would improve integration because a basic pension would be received by all individuals and the superannuation and other long-term savings systems could build upon this foundation without being prejudiced by disincentive effects.

The Institute of Actuaries of Australia (1994) showed that with the introduction of a universal pension, the level of compulsory employer superannuation contributions could be reduced by 3 per cent of earnings while maintaining the same level of net retirement income for most individuals. As noted earlier, the provision of a base pension forms an important component of the retirement income systems in most developed countries.

The complex taxation arrangements are more difficult to resolve. Two alternatives, referred to as Option A and Option B, are presented, Option B representing the more radical approach. These are described in Tables 10.2 and 10.3, using the same format as for Table 10.1 for ease of comparison. The 'purchase price allowance' is the cost of the annuity divided by the expected term of payment (14.6 years for males aged 65), and AWE stands for average weekly earnings.

The Australian government currently receives considerable tax revenue from superannuation funds and, for this budgetary reason, the 15 per cent tax on tax-deductible contributions and fund investment income is retained as a feature of both options.

Option A provides an incentive for all individuals to contribute by removing the very restrictive conditions on the current tax rebate of 10 per cent of contributions. It provides greater encouragement for the use of annuities because the total benefit used to purchase an annuity constitutes a tax-exempt undeducted purchase price. From the individual's perspective, it

Table 10.2: Alternative Tax Structure A

Contribution rates	Employer 6%, employee 3%
Contribution tax	15% on tax-deductible employer contributions
Employee contribution rebate	10% of employee contributions, subject to same age-related maxima (but no other limitations), are refundable. Refund may exceed tax liability
Superannuation fund earnings	Nominal rate of tax of 15% (assumed to be an effective rate of 7.5%, allowing for credits)
Lump sum tax	All lump sum benefits subject to tax schedule: 0% on amounts < 2 × AWE 20% on amounts 2-4 × AWE 35% on amounts > 4 × AWE Medicare levy of 1.4% on all amounts
Age pension	Universal pension, taxable, no means-tests; income tax rebate depending on income
Annuities in payment	Superannuation and other annuities are taxed as income, except that the purchase price allowance is exempt
Superannuation pension rebate	No rebate

Table 10.3: Alternative Tax Structure B

Contribution rates	Employer 6%, employee 3%
Contribution tax	15% on tax deductible employer contributions
Employee contribution rebate	10% of employee contributions refundable. No limitations apply
Superannuation fund earnings	Nominal rate of tax of 15% (assumed to be an effective rate of 7.5%, after allowance for credits)
Lump sum tax	No lump sum tax as such. Total superannuation benefit is subject to tax schedule of: 0% on amounts $< 3 \times$ AWE 20% on amounts 3-10 $\times$ AWE 40% on amounts $> 10 \times$ AWE No Medicare levy
Age pension	Universal pension, taxable, no means-tests; income tax rebate depending on income
Annuities in payment	Superannuation annuities are exempt from tax; other annuities are taxed as income, except that the purchase price allowance is exempt
Superannuation pension rebate	No rebate

is a much simpler system. A rebate is received in respect of member contributions (although age-related maxima on contributions remain), benefits are taxable with a three-tier tax system for lump sum benefits, and pensions are subject to income tax but with a constant annual exemption (representing the purchase price divided by life expectancy at the age when the annuity commences).

Option B simplifies the taxation structure further by abolishing all maxima (whether expressed in terms of contributions or of benefits) and introducing a progressive superannuation benefits tax. This tax, with rates ranging from 0 per cent to 40 per cent, is paid at retirement when the benefit is received by the individual. With these tax rates there is little incentive for excessive benefits to accrue, so maximum benefits can be abolished. Similarly, if the tax structure provides little incentive for very large contributions, there is no need for any restrictions on the size of contributions.

The superannuation tax in Option B is paid on the capital value of the total superannuation benefits received and the tax rate is independent of any other income. Any subsequent annuity payments, generated from the superannuation benefit, are exempt from the tax system. This extreme simplification, with the associated removal of the undeducted purchase price concept, may appear generous. However, under the current system most of an annuity purchased by an amount that has already been subject to lump sum tax is exempt from income tax due to the allowance for the undeducted purchase price. The extension of this exemption to include the total annuity payment is both a simplification and a concession to annuitants who forego access to their capital during the life of the annuity.

There are other advantages in introducing a single tax on all superannuation benefits at the point of retirement. First, it is simple, because the tax is paid on one occasion and no further taxation is needed. Secondly, it is equitable, because all superannuation benefits are treated in the same manner and multiple benefits are easily accounted for since the tax rate applied is independent of other income. Thirdly, it has revenue advantages. The government receives all the superannuation benefits tax at the time of retirement and thus some of the current revenue from the taxation on future pension income is brought forward. Fourthly, there are administrative savings, because pensioners and the tax department no longer need to continue to administer the taxation of annuities.

10.4 The Simulation Model

The core of the simulation model consists of the specification of earnings profiles over the working life for members of a cohort and the determination of the age at death of each simulated individual. These components are described in turn below. This is essentially the model used to examine the earnings-related government pension scheme in the UK in Creedy (1982), and modified to examine taxation in Australia in Cameron and Creedy (1995).

10.4.1 Earnings Profiles

Gross earnings in each year of working life are generated using a model of age-earnings profiles in which earnings in age group t are lognormally distributed as $\Lambda\left(\mu_t, \sigma_t^2\right)$, where μ_t and σ_t^2 are respectively the mean and variance of the logarithms of earnings. For further details of this model and estimation procedures, see Creedy (1985, 1992). These two parameters are assumed to be quadratic and linear functions of t respectively, so that :

$$\mu_t = \mu_1 + (\theta + g)\, t - \delta t^2 \tag{10.8}$$

$$\sigma_t^2 = \sigma_1^2 + \sigma_u^2 t \tag{10.9}$$

where g is the nominal growth rate of earnings. This growth rate is assumed to affect all age groups equally. The five parameters μ_1, σ_1^2, θ, δ and σ_u^2 were estimated using data for Australian males and are $\mu_1 = 9.98064$, $\theta = 0.0385$, $\delta = 0.00086$, $\sigma_1^2 = 0.1817$, $\sigma_u^2 = 0.00575$, and the value of g was set equal to 0.06; for further details of these estimates see Creedy (1992).

10.4.2   Age at Death

The simulations are based on the assumption of differential mortality experience. The age at death in retirement for each individual relates to the lifetime earnings of that individual relative to the whole cohort, incorporating a stochastic component, on the basis of an earnings and mortality distribution derived from available data. The number of years the ith individual survives after retirement, d_i, is obtained, following Creedy (1982), using the following specification:

$$d_i = \bar{d} + \beta \log \frac{\bar{X}_i}{M} + u_i \qquad (10.10)$$

where $\bar{X}_i$ is the individual's annual average real earnings, M is the geometric mean value of the $\bar{X}_i$s, $\bar{d}$ is the average number of years individuals survive after retirement and u_i is a random normal variable $N(0, \sigma_u^2)$. The values used are $\bar{d} = 14.6$, $\beta = 8$ and $\sigma_u^2 = 50$. These values result from a numerical search procedure involving comparisons of the simulated survival curve with the actual survival curve for Australian males.

10.4.3   Economic Assumptions

In producing the simulations, it is necessary to make assumptions about a range of interest and growth rates. The simulated incomes are in nominal terms, since this is appropriate for the application of income taxation. The major assumptions used in the simulation are shown in Table 10.4.

10.5   Some Comparisons

This section compares the alternative schemes in terms of their redistributive impact over the life cycle of a cohort of males, using the simulation model. The Gini inequality measure, based on present values of lifetime income, is used. Other measures were found to give similar results and are therefore not presented here.

This analysis is restricted to the experience of males, as their earnings data are readily available and the pattern of earnings change over the working

Table 10.4: Economic Assumptions

Tax on super fund investment income	7.5%
Tax on savings fund investment income	25%
Annual increase in average earnings	6%
Annual increase in income tax thresholds	5.5%
Annual inflation rate	5%
Gross annual rate of return on super fund	9%
Gross annual return on bank account	5%
The purchase price of retirement annuities	12.5
Annuities escalate in payment at	5%

life may be expected to be reasonably stable. Hence, the earnings distribution and mortality are representative of all Australian males. When calculating the taxation and benefit levels each individual is assumed to have no dependants. It is planned to extend the model to allow for household formation and the more complex labour market experience of females.

Results are presented illustrating the consequences of a number of different decisions made at retirement. It is assumed that superannuation represents the only source of cumulative savings throughout the working life. Five different choices at retirement are examined, as follows.

Choice (i) allows for all of the superannuation benefit to be used for the purchase of an annuity.

Choice (ii) uses 50 per cent of the superannuation benefit to purchase an annuity, and 50 per cent is placed in an interest-bearing bank account.

Choice (iii) also uses 50 per cent of the superannuation benefit to purchase an annuity, but the balance is put to immediate consumption at retirement.

Choice (iv) entails all of the superannuation benefit being taken as a lump sum, then placed in an interest-bearing bank account.

Choice (v) also commutes all the superannuation benefits to a lump sum, but all assets are spent on retirement, so no income provision is made.

Table 10.5: Gini Measures of Lifetime Income

	Current	Option A	Option B
100% annuity	0.2459	0.2455	0.2391
50% annuity 50% bank	0.2303	0.2328	0.2298
50% annuity 50% cash	0.2327	0.2344	0.2313
100% lump sum all to bank	0.2174	0.2185	0.2215
100% lump sum all spent	0.2242	0.2215	0.2244

Table 10.6: Total Tax Ratio

	Current	Option A	Option B
100% annuity	0.1475	0.1327	0.1703
50% annuity 50% bank	0.1457	0.1445	0.1777
50% annuity 50% cash	0.1263	0.1355	0.1716
100% lump sum all to bank	0.1504	0.1689	0.1848
100% lump sum all spent	0.1170	0.1553	0.1745

In the cases where some or all of the superannuation benefit is used to purchase an annuity, this escalates at 5 per cent per annum. Comparison is restricted to whole-life annuities with payments linked to inflation, which are payable throughout the lifetime of the annuitant and leave no residual capital value. The purchase rate used for annuities is 12.5, so that $1,000 purchases an annual lifetime income whose amount is $80 in the first year of payment. This rate is consistent with the long-term economic assumptions used in the simulations and described above.

The interest-bearing account contributes to the assets of the individual to the extent of the balance of the account, and is assessed in the application of the assets means-test associated with the age pension. It is assumed that the account is reduced by annual capital drawings and eventually extinguished, but if the retiree dies during the drawing-down period the balance in the account provides a capital bequest. The amount withdrawn from the account each year is the balance of the account at the start of a year, divided by the number of years outstanding until age 80. The interest which is earned on this account is taxable as income to the individual in the usual way, and is assessable as income in the application of the age pension income means-test.

Comparisons of the Gini measure of inequality of net lifetime income under alternative arrangments are show in Table 10.5. The major result is that, for each method of disposing of the superannuation benefits, the effect on inequality of removing the means-tests on the government pension and simplifying the tax structure is small. The two simplified structures represent substantial reductions in complexity, much of which has arisen from an attempt to introduce some progressivity directly into the structure of superannuation taxation. Nevertheless, the simplifications have a minor effect on inequality. Indeed, the results are more sensitive to the decision made by individuals in choosing how to invest the superannuation benefit; the differences between the rows of Table 10.5 are more substantial than differences between tax structures. Option B raises more lifetime revenue per person, as measured by the ratio of the difference between arithmetic mean present values of gross and net lifetime incomes, divided by gross lifetime income, shown in Table 10.6.

Differential mortality is found to be an important determinant of lifetime inequality. This is particularly marked in the case where the superannuation benefit is used to purchase a whole-life annuity, and arises because the purchase price of annuities is independent of the individual's lifetime income. For example, if instead of differential mortality, all individuals are assumed to live for 14 years after retirement, the progressivity measures rise to 0.3891, 0.4452 and 0.3581 respectively for the current tax structure, Option A and Option B (compared with 0.2573, 0.2961 and 0.2467), while the Gini inequality measures of net lifetime income fall to 0.2145, 0.2142 and 0.2103 respectively (compared with 0.2459, 0.2455 and 0.2391) .

These comparisons assume that superannuation contributions constitute the only savings for retirement. Additional saving typically implies a mixed, but small, effect on inequality. However, the main result is unchanged; the tax and pension simplifications have little effect on the equity measures. The most significant differences arise as a result of the choice of alternative methods of disposing of resources at retirement. Further investigations were carried out to test the sensitivity of this result to the assumptions used. Variations included increasing employer superannuation contributions to 9 per cent for Options A and B to match the employer subsidy available under the current structure, and increasing the level of the basic age pension. In all cases the general result remains unchanged; the significant differences arise from the choice of retirement behaviour rather than from the structure of taxes and benefits. Furthermore, the role of differential mortality is more significant than the differences in structure.

10.6   Conclusions

This chapter discussed the issue of lifetime income equality under alternative retirement income arrangements with particular reference to Australia. The advantage of using that country's experience is that the government-funded age pension is fully means-tested and thereby provides a contrast to nations where part or all of a basic pension is paid to all aged persons. With many governments considering an increase in the level of means-testing, the Australian experience provides valuable insights.

The results showed that the introduction of a universal pension, coupled with significant changes and simplifications to the structure of taxation on superannuation, have very little effect on the redistributive impact of the tax structure in a life-cycle framework. The analysis of lifetime inequality does not find substantial differences in the redistribution of lifetime income associated with means-testing and other features of the taxation system. It is, therefore, not possible to conclude that the use of a universal, rather than means-tested, age pension significantly affects inequality.

Hence, alternative structures for the provision of retirement incomes can be considered which embody hybrids of the current Australian system and other systems in place worldwide, without anticipating that these will necessarily entail significant changes in equity. Similarly, it would seem possible to eliminate complexities from the current system without having any deleterious effect on equity.

It was found that the progressivity of a system is substantially more sensitive to the characteristics of individual behaviour following retirement and the post-retirement mortality experience, than the presence or otherwise of means-tests for the age pension. The following chapter examines this behaviour in more detail.

Chapter 11

Modelling Retirement Decisions

At the time of retirement, individuals in Australia are faced with a complex set of decisions affecting future income provision. This set may reasonably be described as a 'retirement maze'. At the date of retirement taxes are imposed on the individual's accumulated assets, depending on how the individual disposes of them. The tax levied at retirement depends on the source of the accumulated assets, their absolute value and the proportion which is taken as a lump sum. The method of their dispersal also affects the income tax liability of the individual during the retirement years, along with the working of the means-tests which govern the age pension eligibility. Annuities which are purchased using superannuation assets are not taxed in the same way as annuities purchased by other savings, and a larger proportion is disregarded by the age pension means-tests. The details are given in chapter 10.

In addition to the complexity imposed by the tax and benefit structure, subjective values affect priorities. Optimal behaviour for an individual may be defined by different criteria, for example in terms of maximising gross post-retirement income, or net consumption in retirement. The valuation criterion may or may not include the value of any estate remaining at death.

The previous chapter examined inequality measures of alternative tax and benefit structures for a cohort, on the assumption that all individuals follow the same route at retirement. For example, each individual is assumed to expend all assets on the purchase of an annuity, or a specified proportion on

179

annuity purchase and the remainder on consumption. The resulting retirement income experience of members of the cohort is compared for a range of decisions. It was found that, in analysing inequality, there is little to distinguish the results of the different tax and benefit structures examined. The factors which significantly affect equity and progressivity were found to be the choice of route at retirement and, importantly, the mortality experience of the individuals.

However, it is expected that individuals with widely differing earnings histories would make diverse choices at the time of retirement. This chapter modifies to the simulation model to enable each individual to tailor the personal retirement choice to give the optimal retirement consumption stream, measured by a given criterion. In practice, there are two dimensions to the choice problem, as individuals must decide when to retire as well as select the route through the maze. However, the question of alternative retirement ages is addressed in chapter 12.

In the simulations, each individual in a cohort is restricted to one of 47 choices regarding the disposal of accumulated assets at retirement. For each individual, the value of each of these routes is calculated using one of five criteria, and the individual adopts the strategy with the highest value. Hence, in terms of the specified criterion, each individual is considered to optimise the retirement choice.

The aim of this chapter is to examine the effect on intra-cohort equity and progressivity, allowing for optimal individual behaviour at retirement. The criteria involve a set of utility functions based on net consumption in the retirement years, with or without regard to any remaining estate at the time of death. Section 11.1 describes the range of routes available at the time of retirement and the five optimisation criteria. It examines the numbers of individuals choosing each decision under each criterion, using two different mortality assumptions. Section 11.2 presents the results arising from a change in the structure of retirement income policy. Section 11.3 compares the implications for lifetime redistribution of assuming that all members of a cohort make the same choice at retirement with those resulting from the assumption that individual optimisation is exercised.

11.1 Retirement Decisions

As in chapter 10, the simulations used a model of age-earnings profiles estimated for Australian males, over all occupations and household types. When calculating the tax paid during the working life and retirement, and when considering the age pension and its associated means tests, the simulated individuals are, however, treated as if they were single and homeowners. In a more complete analysis it would obviously be desirable to model household formation and joint decision-taking, where appropriate. But it is argued that the present approach is sufficient to demonstrate the complexity of the system in Australia and the nature of the incentive structure created. All individuals are assumed to enter the workforce at age 20 and to retire at age 65. The relevant income tax rates and thresholds used, along with rebate levels, are those operating in Australia in 1994. They are indexed each year using the rates indicated below. Other major economic assumptions used in the simulation are as in Table 10.4.

11.1.1 The Range of Routes Available

At the time of retirement each individual has accumulated assets which may be classified in three ways. First, there is the sum of superannuation contributions arising from employee contributions, assumed to be 3 per cent of gross earnings throughout the working life. Secondly, there are accumulated employer contributions, known as deducted contributions, assumed to be 9 per cent of gross earnings in each year, plus all other investment income earned by the fund. These rates correspond to those recommended for a 'mature' version of current policy in Australia. These are treated in different ways for tax purposes and are known as the undeducted benefit and the taxable benefit respectively. Thirdly, each individual has other accumulated savings; these are assumed to be at the rate of 5 per cent of disposable income in each year. These assets are disposed of at retirement and the initial disposal identifies amounts put to various uses thereafter.

The superannuation assets may initially be used in a combination of two ways. They may be used to purchase a lifetime annuity, or may be taken as a lump sum which is subject to lump sum tax. The other savings, and any superannuation lump sum taken, may be used in one of three ways. The simulations allows for the after-tax cash amounts to be used to purchase an annuity, to be deposited in an interest-bearing bank account, or put to immediate consumption. These three destinations are available in any combination. Any annuities purchased are identified throughout retirement according to the source of the money which is used to purchase them. This distinction governs the income tax rules which apply to them, and also the treatment under the operation of the age pension means tests. Annuities purchased by lump sum proceeds from the superannuation benefit are treated in the same way as annuities purchased from other savings; both are considered to be purchased by after-tax money. The model allows for two basic methods of retirement income provision, the money purchase method, and the defined benefit method. In the former method, a proportion of the available amount used to purchase an annuity is specified, and in the latter method a level of income to be purchased is specified. Defined benefit levels are described as a proportion of the average of the final three years' earnings before retirement.

After the purchase of annuities from pre- or post-tax money, an amount may be placed in an interest-bearing bank account; the amount is specified as a proportion of the money available. The account attracts taxable interest payments at a constant rate, and is subject to annual drawings. The amount withdrawn at the end of each year is assumed to be the balance of the account divided by the number of years remaining to age 80, so the account is extinguished at age 80. This is an arbitrary assumption, but it is made in the absence of an explicit model of both bequest behaviour and the formation of expectations of length of life. As individuals do not know how long they will live, it is possible that they will die leaving some money in the bank account, which provides a bequest. Hence bequests can exist in some cases, but they are not modelled as a deliberate decision of individuals. The final allocation at the time of retirement is to consumption. All money remaining after the above provisions for income and investment is spent immediately.

Given the complexity of the maze of choices, there is in principle an infinitely large number of routes which may be taken at retirement. In this chapter a catalogue of 47 available routes through the maze has been constructed. The routes over which each individual makes the optimal choice are described in Tables 11.1 and 11.2. In Table 11.1, column 2 indicates the first call on the use of pre-tax superannuation assets. The initials 'LS' signify that the superannuation assets are taken entirely as a lump sum. Where this is given as 'A' the superannuation assets are used to provide an annuity to the defined level of income described in column 4. If the superannuation assets are insufficient to purchase an annuity to the required level, then savings are drawn upon until the level is reached. Any balance of pre-tax money is then taken as a lump sum, and added to other post-tax money. If there is insufficient money to purchase the defined level of income, the individual buys as much as possible, so that all assets are devoted to annuity purchase.

In Table 11.2, column 2 indicates the percentage of pre-tax superannuation assets used to purchase an annuity. The balance of superannuation assets is taken as a lump sum and later pooled with any balance of the savings accumulation. If the superannuation assets are converted entirely to a lump sum, as in routes 35-47 inclusive, then the post-tax money is added to the savings accumulation and the stated percentage applied to the purchase of an annuity. Thus route 35 specifies that all superannuation is taken as a lump sum and all the money then available is used to buy an annuity. Route 25 specifies that all benefits are used to purchase annuities, but one annuity arises from pre-tax superannuation assets while the other arises from post-tax savings and therefore involves a different tax and age pension treatment.

The route with the highest value for the specified criterion is chosen by an individual. If there is more than one route with the same value, the highest route number is preferred.

11.1.2 Individual Evaluation of Routes

There are many ways to evaluate the results of a given route. Since this chapter is concerned with the consequences of action at the time of retirement, the evaluation criteria relate only to experience after that time. Any

Table 11.1: Routes 1-24: Defined Benefit Cases

Route	Super pre-tax destination	Savings and post-tax destination	Defined benefit: % of final salary	% of balance to bank	% of balance to consump
1	A	A	85	-	100
2	A	A	75	-	100
3	A	A	65	100	0
4	A	A	65	50	50
5	A	A	65	-	100
6	LS	A	65	100	-
7	LS	A	65	50	50
8	LS	A	65	-	100
9	LS	A	60	-	100
10	A	A	50	100	-
11	A	A	50	50	50
12	A	A	50	-	100
13	LS	A	50	100	-
14	LS	A	50	50	50
15	LS	A	50	-	100
16	LS	A	45	-	100
17	A	A	35	100	-
18	A	A	35	50	50
19	A	A	35	-	100
20	LS	A	35	100	-
21	LS	A	35	50	50
22	LS	A	35	-	100
23	A	A	25	-	100
24	A	A	10	-	100

Table 11.2: Routes 25-47: Money Purchase Cases

Route	% of super to annuity	% of Savings and post-tax to annuity	% of balance to bank	% of balance to consump
25	100	100	0	0
26	100	0	100	0
27	100	0	50	50
28	100	0	0	100
29	50	50	100	0
30	50	50	50	50
31	50	50	0	100
32	50	0	100	0
33	50	0	50	50
34	50	0	0	100
35	LS	100	0	0
36	LS	85	100	0
37	LS	70	100	0
38	LS	70	50	50
39	LS	50	100	0
40	LS	50	50	50
41	LS	50	0	100
42	LS	0	100	0
43	LS	0	75	25
44	LS	0	50	50
45	LS	0	25	75
46	LS	0	10	90
47	LS	0	0	100

pre-retirement income or expenditure is independent of the retirement choice, and is therefore ignored. Results have been obtained for optimised behaviour for each of five different evaluation criteria. The valuations are all based on present values at the time of entry to the workforce.

All criteria are defined in terms of a utility function based on net consumption in each year of retirement. Individuals are assumed not to save from any disposable income during retirement. The amount of net consumption in any year is the sum of income from any purchased annuities, plus the age pension received where relevant, plus the amount taken from the bank account, less the amount of income tax paid, allowing for the appropriate rebates due. This amount is not the same, in general, as the net income in the year. Net income includes the interest earned on the bank account, but does not include the capital amount withdrawn from it. Some of the criteria used take into account the value of the bequest, if any. This is the balance of the bank account at the time of death. Since the bank account is zero by age 80, the bequest is zero for any individual who survives this age.

The criteria are set out in Table 11.3. The expressions in Table 11.3 are slightly simplified, as in calculating the present values consumption is assumed to occur uniformly throughout the year, and the bequest is valued at the end of the year of death. If $c(t)$ is the net consumption in year t, the working life begins at age 20 when $t = 0$, retirement begins at the end of year $t = 45$, at age 65, death occurs in year d and the interest rate is denoted by i, Criterion 1 involves an additive utility function with utility in each period simply a linear function of consumption.

It is desirable to allow for decreasing marginal utility, and this is done in two ways. First, each period's utility is a logarithmic function of consumption, and secondly, consumption is raised to some power, α $(0 < \alpha < 1)$. The utility function used by Criterion 2 is the sum over the retirement years of the present value of the logarithm of net retirement consumption plus the bequest. Criterion 3 is the same as Criterion 2 but with no allowance for the bequest. Criterion 4 is the sum of the present values of net consumption raised to the power α, where the bequest is included. Criterion 5 is the same as Criterion 4, but with no allowance for the bequest.

Table 11.3: Alternative Criteria

No.	Criterion
1	$\sum_{t=46}^{d} (1+i)^{-t} c(t) + b(1+i)^{-d}$
2	$\sum_{t=46}^{d} (1+i)^{-t} \log c(t) + (1+i)^{-d} \log b$
3	$\sum_{t=46}^{d} (1+i)^{-t} \log c(t)$
4	$\sum_{t=46}^{d} (1+i)^{-t} c(t)^{\alpha} + (1+i)^{-d} b^{\alpha}$
5	$\sum_{t=46}^{d} (1+i)^{-t} c(t)^{\alpha}$

In the following simulations the value of α is set at 0.25. This means that a 1 per cent increase in consumption is equivalent to a 0.25 per cent increase in utility. In the logarithmic case a 1 per cent increase in consumption gives rise to an increase in utility of $1/\log(c)$ per cent. Decreasing marginal utility implies that individuals prefer a more stable consumption stream, other things being equal. Hence, it is less likely that consuming all assets at retirement, and then living on the full age pension, will be optimal. This implication is clearly shown in the simulation results.

11.1.3 Optimal Choice of Route

The simulation model was used to simulate the lifetime experience of each of 3,000 individuals. In each case the value of each criterion was evaluated for each of the 47 routes through the maze, and the route giving the maximum value of the relevant criterion was recorded. The simulation was repeated for the assumption of common mortality, such that all individuals live for 14 years after retirement, and for differential mortality whereby the relatively rich live, on average, relatively longer (and the expectation of life at retirement for the median individual is 14 years). The routes giving the maximum values for each criterion are shown in Tables 11.4 and 11.5. For example, the first column of the body of the table shows the number of times each route gives the maximum value using criterion 1, when differential mortality applies.

Tables 11.4 and 11.5 show, not surprisingly, that the optimal route is sensitive both to the criterion used and whether or not there is differential mortality. It is necessary at this point to stress that the evaluation of each

Table 11.4: Optimal Routes (3,000 Individuals)

	Differential mortality					Common mortality				
Route	1	2	3	4	5	1	2	3	4	5
1	4	24	29	19	23	2	37	40	42	44
2	3	16	18	13	15	1	33	33	34	39
3	-	-	-	-	-	-	-	-	-	-
4	-	5	-	7	-	-	15	4	23	-
5	2	12	15	7	11	7	26	27	28	33
6										
7	-	181	82	139	29	-	454	371	327	190
8	65	183	483	201	520	6	274	331	339	476
9	38	88	189	100	205	3	167	170	199	205
10	-	-	-	-	-	-	-	-	-	-
11	-	10	-	7	-	-	4	2	22	-
12	6	1	7	2	7	50	3	4	4	6
13	-	-	-	-	-	-	-	-	-	-
14	-	115	6	100	1	-	32	17	19	4
15	49	55	122	63	171	-	93	105	129	136
16	68	18	73	13	65	-	34	34	46	47
17	-	-	-	-	-	-	-	-	-	-
18	-	-	-	2	-	-	-	-	1	-
19	39	-	14	-	12	167	1	1	1	1
20	-	-	-	-	-	-	-	-	-	-
21	-	99	1	98	-	-	8	6	5	1
22	219	1	32	2	54	-	2	3	6	8
23	94	-	15	-	24	502	-	-	-	-
24	579	-	12	-	38	1872	-	-	-	-

Table 11.5: Optimal Routes (3,000 Individuals)

Route	Differential mortality					Common mortality				
	1	2	3	4	5	1	2	3	4	5
25	265	305	309	319	322	-	172	192	14	179
26	-	-	-	-	-	-	-	-	-	-
27	-	10	6	9	1	-	8	-	130	-
28	-	-	13	-	20	-	-	-	-	-
29	-	-	-	-	-	-	-	-	-	-
30	-	3	-	2	-	-	-	-	-	-
31	-	-	-	-	-	-	-	-	-	-
32	-	-	-	-	-	-	-	-	-	-
33	-	-	-	-	-	-	-	-	-	-
34	4	-	1	-	-	51	-	-	-	-
35	160	609	635	581	593	1	170	276	34	162
36	-	-	-	-	-	-	-	-	-	-
37	-	-	-	-	-	-	-	-	-	-
38	-	559	651	410	510	-	1467	1384	1597	1469
39	-	-	-	-	-	-	-	-	-	-
40	-	150	6	132	2	-	-	-	-	-
41	135	-	86	-	152	4	-	-	-	-
42	1	1	-	1	-	-	-	-	-	-
43	3	168	-	276	-	-	-	-	-	-
44	52	247	-	357	-	-	-	-	-	-
45	156	128	-	128	-	-	-	-	-	-
46	36	12	-	12	-	-	-	-	-	-
47	1022	0	195	-	225	334	-	-	-	-

route for each individual is *ex post*. The criteria refer to the consumption stream and bequest actually received by the individual over the whole of the retirement period. These results do not therefore directly indicate which routes are optimal *ex ante*, since it would be necessary to model explicitly the formation of expectations about the length of life. The two concepts coincide only if individuals know at retirement how long they will live; Hammermesh (1985) examined the substantial differences between expectations and actual longevity for a sample of individuals in the US.

The effect of allowing for decreasing marginal utility of consumption, irrespective of the form of the specification, is dramatic. With differential mortality and criterion 1, route 47 is optimal for one-third of the individuals, where all assets are converted to a lump sum and consumed at retirement. With common mortality and criterion 1, almost two-thirds of individuals have route 24 as the optimal route, where an annuity of only 10 per cent of final salary is purchased at retirement and all other assets are consumed. In practice, such consumption may of course involve the purchase of durable goods which provide a flow of consumption benefits, but this aspect is not modelled here. With decreasing marginal utility (criteria 2-5), route 38 is optimal for almost one-half of individuals when there is common mortality. This route involves taking all superannuation assets in a lump sum, and using 70 per cent of the sum of the post-tax value and savings to purchase an annuity, with the remainder divided between a bank account and consumption. With differential mortality, there is a much wider spread of optimal routes. Under all criteria, about half of the cohort has an optimal route that is a defined benefit case, and approximately half has an optimal choice among the lump sum money purchase routes 35-47.

The question arises of the 'cost' of making a sub-optimal decision, involving a comparison of the value of each criterion for each route. With 47 routes and 3,000 individuals, it is difficult to summarise such information. For example, a comparison may show that one route has a higher average value (for a given criterion) than another route; but the latter may actually be chosen by relatively more people, depending on the joint distributions involved. However, using just three representative individuals and a small number of alternative routes, Atkinson *et al.* (1995) showed that substantial differences in the present values of consumption can arise.

11.2 The Effect of Policy Changes

The results of the previous section have shown that the superannuation taxation and age pension system in Australia do not appear to provide a clear incentive for individuals to purchase retirement income streams from their superannuation assets at retirement. The optimal *ex post* decisions were found to be spread over a range of choices, many of which involved taking superannuation assets in the form of a lump sum. This section examines two policy structures as alternatives to the one currently operating.

The major motivation behind the proposals is to simplify the huge complexity discussed earlier. Each alternative represents a more radical simplification, and incorporates features common in other countries (such as the provision of a universal pension). Australia is unusual in allowing superannuation benefits to be taken in the form of a lump sum. It is likely that this will become a sensitive policy issue, but the alternatives considered below stop short of preventing the taking of lump sums. Instead, they impose a revised tax structure.

11.2.1 Alternative Structures

The two alternative structures are referred to as Option A and Option B, and offer progressively radical simplifications. The major characteristics of the current scheme and the alternatives are summarised in chapter 10. Both alternatives involve a reduced level of employer contribution, and a simplified rebate structure for employee's contributions. These and the other major differences in structure represent elements of the current debate on retirement incomes policy. Both options provide a universal pension during retirement and a simplified taxation schedule for the superannuation benefits. The low-income earners rebate remains in place. Option A taxes annuities in receipt as income in the same way regardless of their source. Option B exacts all superannuation taxation at the time of retirement, and superannuation annuities in payment are exempt from income tax.

11.2.2   Results of Optimal Choices

The results of simulating the experience of 3,000 individuals for the two options are shown in Tables 11.6 and 11.7, for the assumptions of differential mortality and common mortality respectively. Routes which are not chosen by any individuals are omitted from these tables. It can be seen that these reforms have a dramatic effect on the allocation of routes through the retirement maze. In particular, the optimal route *ex post* is route 25 in many more cases, particularly for option B. This is the route that involves the use of all superannuation and savings to purchase an annuity.

Under an assumption of differential mortality, one of the striking effects of Option A, and to a slightly lesser extent Option B, is that routes involving the use of a lump sum are rarely optimal. Option B does not tax lump sums *per se*, but does provide for tax-exempt superannuation annuities. Both options, through the provision of the universal pension, avoid the clustering of optimal routes around margins of the age pension income means-test (routes 22-24 in particular). About 40 per cent of the cohort chooses route 25, irrespective of criterion of valuation as opposed to about 10 per cent under the current scheme. Route 25, the 100 per cent annuity purchase choice, is far more effectively targeted by Options A and B.

Table 11.7 presents the results based on common mortality experience, and survival to 14 years after retirement. The most popular route under the current scheme is route 38, which takes all superannuation as a lump sum, uses 70 per cent on annuity purchase and divides the remainder between the bank investment and consumption. This choice is probably driven by the income means-test. Here the polarising effect is even more marked for Option B, with far more, between about 50 and 80 per cent, selecting route 25 as optimal. Option A, except for valuation criterion 1, results in route 25 being the most popular optimal route.

Importantly, Options A and B both concentrate optimal choices in routes

Table 11.6: Optimal Routes with Differential Mortality

Route	Alternative A					Alternative B				
	1	2	3	4	5	1	2	3	4	5
1	23	156	291	127	265		64	120	47	91
2	37	139	285	124	248	4	87	170	62	130
4		157	4	148	1		66	8	49	2
5	91	117	285	102	267	3	109	223	74	200
8								6		6
9							1	23	1	13
11		176	14	183	1		156	67	101	29
12	200	61	170	55	203	6	87	274	67	262
15								20		14
16			1				36			27
18		100	3	131	2		115	40	103	27
19	212		33		57	8	43	131	34	134
22								23		31
23	152		19		28	1	2	40	2	49
24	95		15		25			22		36
25	1110	1080	1151	1119	1181	1485	1227	1323	1325	1405
27		437	106	350	38		248	58	217	24
28	58		388		410			145		177
30		23		12			33		18	
31			13		12					8
33		78		93						
34	122		25		30			21		32
38							2			
41								29		25
42	183	183		183		190	190		190	
43	10	160		201		5	425		528	
44	8	133		172		18	145		182	
45	28					25				
46	19					10				
47	652		197		232	1244		221		278

Table 11.7: Optimal Routes with Common Mortality

Route	Alternative A					Alternative B				
	1	2	3	4	5	1	2	3	4	5
1	123	484	503	495	520	28	217	217	214	214
2	146	424	445	455	473	35	284	295	289	294
4		133	52	88	6		138	44	87	3
5	395	339	386	397	456	84	328	373	352	378
8							2	2	2	2
9			1				6	7	6	7
11		125	43	116	22		261	84	147	7
12	880	133	154	158	189	150	284	326	311	343
15							2	2	2	2
16							2	2	2	2
18		11	6	13	4		150	46	76	10
19	703	4	5	5	10	131	106	125	115	137
23	169					24	5	5	5	5
25	1	751	1245	510	1123	2474	1254	1471	1391	1595
27		596	159	763	196		6		1	
28	32		1		1	73		1		1
31	2									
34	549									
35						1				

which provide a high level of annuity. Generally the attraction of routes with high levels of immediate consumption are screened out by the assumption of common mortality, and options involving simple bank deposits have little advantage.

The primary result is clear. Both options are more effective at targeting behaviour towards the choice of purchasing annuities under the various sets of assumptions presented here. However, Option B also results in the high-consumption route 47 being optimal for markedly more individuals under certain conditions and valuation criterion. None of the lump sum routes 36-41 is optimal for any of the 3,000 individuals for options A and B when there is differential mortality, and with common mortality routes 29-47 are optimal for very few individuals. Lump sum routes 6-9 and 13-16 are optimal for many individuals in the current scheme, but for very few in options A and B. Route 12, involving an annuity of one half of final salary, is much more frequent with options A and B than with the current scheme. Those choosing lump sum routes 42-46 under the differential mortality assumption appear to do so because value is put on the bequest arising from the bank account balance at death.

Given the government objective of encouraging the use of income streams in retirement, the results suggest that these reforms are worthy of serious consideration. The alternative structures imply a different timing of tax payments over the life cycle. Hence the time stream of total government tax revenue is affected. However, the present model, in dealing with a single cohort of individuals, is not designed to examine the aggregate revenue implications.

11.3 Lifetime Redistribution

The previous two sections examined optimal routes through the retirement maze under the current Australian system and under two alternative systems. This section turns to the question of lifetime redistribution. The analyses reported in chapter 10 concentrated on examining alternative systems where all individuals are assumed to follow a common route. This assumption is relaxed here. Redistribution and tax progressivity are examined for the three tax structures on the assumption that each individual selects at retirement the route which is *ex post* optimal, for each criterion. While this is a strong assumption, it is useful to make comparisons with the case where all individuals take the same route. Before presenting simulation results, the summary measures used are briefly described.

11.3.1   Summary Measures

This subsection defines the various summary measures of redistribution and progressivity used. A basic concept is that of the well-known Lorenz curve. If individuals are ranked in ascending order according to their pre-tax incomes, denoted x_i, the Lorenz curve is defined as the relationship between the proportion of people and the associated proportion of total income obtained by those individuals. Both axes therefore vary from 0 to 1 and if all individuals have the same income, the Lorenz curve is a $45°$ line. The Gini measure of inequality is a measure of the distance of the Lorenz curve from the line of equal distribution. It is twice the area contained by the Lorenz curve and the $45°$ line; the area is doubled simply to ensure that the maximum value that the Gini measure can take is 1.

It is more useful for practical purposes to have a mathematical expression of this area, rather than rely on a geometrical approach. In the case of the distribution of pre-tax income, x, where the incomes are arranged in ascending order, the Gini measure, G_x, can be calculated using:

$$G_x = 1 + \frac{1}{N} - \frac{2}{N^2} \sum_{i=1}^{N} (N + 1 - i) \left(\frac{x_i}{\bar{x}} \right) \tag{11.1}$$

However, for present purposes it is most conveniently expressed in terms of the following covariance:

$$G_x = \left(\frac{2}{\bar{x}} \right) Cov\left(x, F(x) \right) \tag{11.2}$$

where $F(x)$ is the distribution function of income, so that $F(x)$ represents the proportion of individuals with incomes less than or equal to x, and $\bar{x}$ is the arithmetic mean pre-tax income; see Yitzhaki (1983).

Suppose that the tax and transfer system is such that net or post-tax income, y, is given by:

$$y = x - t(x) \tag{11.3}$$

It is possible to obtain a Lorenz curve and corresponding Gini measure of inequality of net income, G_y, by substituting y for x in equation (11.2). The redistributive effect of the tax system can be measured using the Reynolds-Smolensky measure, L, given by the difference between the two Gini measures, so that:

$$L = G_x - G_y \tag{11.4}$$

The redistributive impact and the progressivity of a tax system are different concepts, since the latter is defined to reflect the disproportionality of tax payments. It is useful to define a type of Lorenz curve in which the individuals are ordered according to their pre-tax incomes. The proportion of people is then related to the corresponding proportion of total post-tax income obtained by those individuals. This type of curve is called a concentration curve. This is not the same as the Lorenz curve of post-tax income because the tax system may lead to a re-ranking of individuals when moving from the pre-tax to the post-tax distribution.

The concentration curve gives rise to an area measure that is very similar to the Gini inequality measure, but is for obvious reasons called the concentration index. Hence, if the ranking of individuals by x is maintained, the concentration index of net income, C_y, is given by:

$$C_y = \left(\frac{2}{\bar{y}}\right) Cov\left(y, F(x)\right) \tag{11.5}$$

Similarly, it is possible to plot the proportion of people against the corresponding proportion of total tax paid by those individuals, when the individuals are also ranked in ascending order according to their pre-tax incomes. This gives rise to a tax concentration curve that can be plotted in the same diagram as the Lorenz curve of pre-tax income and the concentration curve of net income. The associated tax concentration index, C_t, may be obtained by substituting the arithmetic mean amount of tax paid, $\bar{t}$, for $\bar{y}$ and $t(x)$ for y in (11.5). Hence it is given by:

$$C_t = \left(\frac{2}{\bar{t}}\right) Cov\left(t(x), F(x)\right) \qquad (11.6)$$

If the tax system is proportional, so that $t(x) = tx$ for all x, the concentration curve of taxation and the Lorenz curve of pre-tax income coincide. The curves differ if there is a degree of disproportionality in the tax system. If the tax system is progressive, the concentration curve of taxation shows more inequality than the Lorenz curve of pre-tax income. Kakwani's measure of disproportionality or progressivity, K, is defined as the difference between the tax concentration index and the Gini measure of x. Hence:

$$K = C_t - G_x \qquad (11.7)$$

In a cross-sectional context, there is no reason why the ranking of individuals should be different when using pre-tax and post-tax incomes, if there are no non-income differences in the tax structure. However, re-ranking can occur in a life-cycle framework because of the variability in incomes from year to year, if marginal tax rates vary with income. If two individuals have the same present value of gross lifetime income, but one individual has a more variable income stream over time than another, the person with the variable stream pays a higher present value of tax over the period. It has been suggested that a requirement of horizontal equity is that individuals with the same pre-tax lifetime income should have the same net income. Therefore, the re-ranking of individuals when moving from the distribution of x to that of y provides a measure of horizontal inequity. The Atkinson-Plotnick index, P, measures this using:

$$P = \frac{G_y - C_y}{2G_y} \qquad (11.8)$$

The concentration measure, C_y, involves ranking by x and the Gini inequality measure, G_y, involves ranking by y, so an absence of re-ranking implies that $P = 0$.

The various measures defined above can be related to each other using an explicit formula; this is not surprising given the reliance of the measures on the basic concept of the Lorenz curve. Define the effective total tax ratio, g, as the ratio of the total tax paid to the total pre-tax income. In the life-cycle framework, the value of g is the difference between the present values of gross and net income divided by the present value of gross income over all individuals. An important relationship between the various measures is:

$$G_x - G_y = K \left\{ \frac{g}{1-g} \right\} - 2G_y P \qquad (11.9)$$

Thus the redistributive effect of the tax and transfer system, $G_x - G_y$, is proportional to its progressivity, K, less a term that depends on the extent of horizontal inequity; see Lambert (1993). An implication of this result is that a change in the tax and transfer system which increases tax progressivity need not necessarily reduce the Gini inequality of net income. It should be stressed that this approach assumes that the pre-tax distribution is not affected by the tax system, and this assumption is made in the simulation model used here.

11.3.2 Simulation Results

For comparison purposes, Tables 11.8 and 11.9 show, for differential mortality and common mortality respectively, the implications of having each individual follow a common route through the maze. Results are given for five alternative routes, representing substantial differences in the type of choice. The income concept used is the present value of lifetime consumption.

Re-ranking only occurs to any significant extent when there is an assumption of differential mortality. Generally, the results show that there is little effect on the Gini inequality measures in moving from the current scheme to either of options A or B. There is a slight fall in the Kakwani progressivity measure, associated with a slight rise in the tax ratio. Options A and B produce a more stable value for the Kakwani measure over the range of routes, compared with the current scheme. The current structure thus appears to have progressivity implications which are more sensitive to

Table 11.8: Lifetime Progressivity: Differential Mortality and Uniform Choice

Choice	Kakwani			Redistribution		
	Current	Option A	Option B	Current	Option A	Option B
25	0.2134	0.2504	0.2171	0.2509	0.2500	0.2441
32	0.3015	0.3006	0.2486	0.2302	0.2318	0.2295
34	0.3570	0.3212	0.2582	0.2329	0.2346	0.2315
42	0.3473	0.3100	0.2680	0.2171	0.2176	0.2206
47	0.4359	0.3341	0.2792	0.2243	0.2216	0.2245

Choice	Total Tax Ratio			Atkinson-Plotnick		
	Current	Option A	Option B	Current	Option A	Option B
25	0.1599	0.1438	0.1782	0.0109	0.0121	0.0104
32	0.1613	0.1587	0.1908	0.0046	0.0053	0.0046
34	0.1350	0.1443	0.0055	0.1804	0.0059	0.0050
42	0.1669	0.1826	0.1983	0.0014	0.0019	0.0020
47	0.1257	0.1640	0.1833	0.0021	0.0022	0.0025

route choice. However, this effect is linked to the changes in the tax ratio which, under the current scheme, is much lower for the high consumption route 47 than for the annuity choice, route 25. The major difference between the results reflect the differences between the routes selected and whether or not differential mortality is assumed. Although the reforms A and B involve major departures from the current system, they do not appear, other things being equal, to involve significant changes in regressivity or inequality in terms of lifetime consumption.

The results of allowing individuals to make optimal choices, for each criterion and tax structure, are shown in Tables 11.10 and 11.11 for differential mortality and common mortality respectively. For comparison purposes, all measures are based on the same income concept, that is, the present value of lifetime consumption. Again the Gini measure of inequality shows little difference between the tax structures, though it increases slightly in moving from the current scheme to option A. Progressivity falls in moving from the current scheme to option A, and then to B, but this reduction is very small and may be associated with the concommitant increase in the tax ratio. The

Table 11.9: Lifetime Progressivity: Common Mortality and Uniform Choice

Choice		Kakwani	
	Current	OptionA	OptionB
25	0.3616	0.4218	0.3442
32	0.3924	0.4024	0.3319
34	0.4796	0.4376	0.3409
42	0.4042	0.3673	0.3211
47	0.5257	0.4018	0.3392

Choice	Redistribution			Total Tax Ratio		
	Current	Option A	Option B	Current	Option A	Option B
25	0.2135	0.2124	0.2107	0.1671	0.1487	0.1797
32	0.2096	0.2097	0.2094	0.1630	0.1595	0.1878
34	0.2102	0.2112	0.2108	0.1366	0.1460	0.1809
42	0.2068	0.2060	0.2084	0.1639	0.1790	0.1948
47	0.2115	0.2081	0.2107	0.1241	0.1624	0.1817

Table 11.10: Lifetime Progressivity: Differential Mortality and Optimal Choice

	Kakwani			Redistribution		
Crit	Current	Option A	Option B	Current	Option A	Option B
1	0.4517	0.3572	0.2827	0.2317	0.2381	0.2423
2	0.3754	0.3334	0.2727	0.2333	0.2398	0.2424
3	0.3441	0.3081	0.2529	0.2361	0.2425	0.2425
4	0.3881	0.3385	0.2749	0.2325	0.2393	0.2424
5	0.3576	0.3168	0.2577	0.2350	0.2416	0.2425

	Total Tax Ratio			Atkinson-Plotnick		
Crit	Current	Option A	Option B	Current	Option A	Option B
1	0.1104	0.1251	0.1576	0.0037	0.0066	0.0060
2	0.1287	0.1303	0.1615	0.0085	0.0077	0.0068
3	0.1343	0.1345	0.1665	0.0073	0.0090	0.0083
4	0.1259	0.1293	0.1607	0.0052	0.0075	0.0066
5	0.1314	0.1329	0.1652	0.0065	0.0085	0.0079

Table 11.11: Lifetime Progressivity: Common Mortality and Optimal Choice

	Kakwani			Redistribution		
Crit	Current	Option A	Option B	Current	Option A	Option B
1	0.5415	0.4385	0.3441	0.2109	0.2128	0.2107
2	0.4483	0.4237	0.3438	0.2068	0.2125	0.2107
3	0.4484	0.4234	0.3439	0.2067	0.2124	0.2107
4	0.4503	0.4240	0.3439	0.2071	0.2125	0.2107
5	0.4515	0.4238	0.3440	0.2068	0.2125	0.2107

	Total Tax Ratio		
Crit	Current	Option A	Option B
1	0.1218	0.1432	0.1796
2	0.1502	0.1480	0.1797
3	0.1503	0.1481	0.1797
4	0.1492	0.1478	0.1797
5	0.1493	0.1479	0.1797

tax ratios are, as expected, slightly lower when individuals follow optimal choices. The major result seems to continue to hold in these more extensive comparisons; that is, the tax structure alternatives have little effect on redistribution and the results are more sensitive to the assumption of differential mortality.

11.4   Conclusions

This chapter presented simulation results, using a modified version of the simulation model in chapter 10, of allowing individuals to optimise their retirement behaviour under various conditions. It was found that the current structure of taxation and retirement income provision does not provide a clear incentive to purchase annuities, under either an assumption of common mortality experience after retirement or differential mortality experience.

Alternative schemes incorporating a universal pension were found to polarise optimal behaviour away from choices which provide low levels of income, and which are driven by the means test. It was also shown that the current scheme has no clear advantage over these alternatives in terms of equality or progressivity.

The behaviour which proves most valuable to individuals depends very largely on their accurate assessment of the number of years they survive after retirement. Other schemes providing a universal pension are more successful in providing incentives to purchase annuities than the current one, and imply a lower penalty to those whose mortality experience is higher, typically those with lower lifetime earnings.

Chapter 12

The Choice of Early Retirement Age

Individuals approaching retirement are faced with a dual decision problem concerning both the age at which to retire and the manner in which to allocate accumulated assets. The complexity of the system makes it difficult to disentangle the incentive structure influencing the dual decision.

By considering the implications of a large number of routes through the retirement maze in Australia, using alternative evaluation criteria, chapter 11 examined a set of optimal choices for a simulated population on the assumption that each individual retires at age 65. The assets modelled consisted of accumulated superannuation contributions (from employers and employees) made over the working life as part of the Superannuation Guarantee Charge (SGC) along with any additional private savings. The population group consisted of a large number of males in a single cohort, assuming that the scheme is fully mature. It was found, for example, that there is very little incentive inherent in the tax and age pension system for individuals to use their assets to purchase annuities. The government's stated objective in introducing compulsory superannuation was, however, to encourage the private provision of retirement incomes in order to reduce reliance on the means-tested age pension.

The purpose of this chapter is to extend the previous analysis to allow for the retirement age to vary between the ages of 55 and 65 years. The analysis does not allow for the transition to part-time work, and retirement is treated

205

as being irreversible and total. Although voluntary early retirement may affect longevity, this type of interdependence is also ignored. The standard form of labour supply model in a multi-period context is of little value in this context, given the complexity of the tax and transfer system.

The simulation model enables, for each of 11 retirement ages, 46 different routes through the 'retirement maze' to be evaluated in terms of lifetime utility; the best combination for each individual of the 506 alternatives of age and routes is then selected. Working an extra year involves giving up leisure in favour of work in return for extra consumption during that year and following years, as a result of the further accumulation of assets. This may perhaps suggest a simple marginal condition in terms of the equality of marginal utility from an extra year of work and that from an extra year of leisure. However, such a simple flow condition is not operational in this context.

The analysis focuses on two main questions. First, to what extent does the system in Australia, in its mature form, offer an incentive for individuals to retire early? Secondly, to what extent is the decision at retirement regarding the use of assets affected by the retirement age?

All individuals are assumed to enter the workforce at age 20 and no deaths are assumed to occur before age 65. Results are obtained both under the assumption that all individuals live for the same length of time, until age 79, and on the assumption that there is a process of differential mortality. The latter process is such that, on average, those with higher annual average lifetime earnings live relatively longer, following the specification described in chapter 10.

Each accumulates assets at the time of retirement which may be classified in three ways. First, there is the sum of superannuation contributions arising from employee contributions, assumed to be 3 per cent of gross earnings throughout the working life. Secondly, there are accumulated employer contributions, known as deducted contributions, assumed to be 9 per cent of gross earnings in each year, plus all other investment income earned by the fund. These contribution rates correspond to those recommended for a mature version of current policy and have bipartisan political support. These two components are treated in different ways for tax purposes and are known as the undeducted benefit and the taxable benefit respectively. Thirdly, each individual has other accumulated savings; these are assumed to be made at the rate of 5 per cent of disposable income in each year. These assets are disposed of at retirement, and the initial disposal identifies amounts put to various uses thereafter. Further details are given in chapter 10.

The retirement options, or routes through the maze, are described in section 12.1 along with the objective function and the treatment of annuity rates. Simulation results are presented in section 12.2

12.1 Retirement Decisions

12.1.1 The Range of Routes Available

The superannuation assets may initially be used in a combination of two ways. They may be used to purchase a lifetime annuity or may be taken as a lump-sum which is subject to lump sum tax. The other savings, and any superannuation lump sum taken, may be used in one of three ways. The simulation model allows for the after-tax cash amounts to be used to purchase an annuity, to be deposited in an interest-bearing bank account, or to be put to immediate consumption. These three destinations are available in any combination and to various degrees. Any annuities purchased are identified throughout retirement according to the source of the money which is used to purchase them. This distinction governs the income tax rules which apply to them, and also the treatment under the operation of the age pension means tests. Annuities purchased by lump-sum proceeds from the superannuation benefit are treated in the same way as annuities purchased from other savings; both are considered to be purchased by after-tax money.

The simulation model allows for two basic methods of retirement income provision: the money purchase method and the defined benefit method. In the former, a proportion of the available amount used to purchase an annuity is specified, and in the latter, a level of required income is specified. Defined benefit levels are described as a proportion of the average of the final three years' earnings before retirement.

After the purchase of annuities from pre- or post-tax money, an amount may be placed in an interest-bearing bank account; the amount is specified as a proportion of the money available. The account attracts taxable interest payments at a constant rate, and is subject to annual drawings. The amount withdrawn at the end of each year is calculated as the balance of the account divided by the number of years remaining to age 80; thus the account is assumed to be extinguished at age 80. This is an arbitrary assumption, but it is made in the absence of an explicit model of bequest behaviour and the formation of expectations of length of life. This assumption approximates to the conditions governing the draw-down of allocated pensions and provides an appropriate alternative to the other choices available here. As individuals do not know how long they will live, it is possible that they will die leaving some money in the bank account, in which case this provides a bequest. Hence, bequests exist in some cases, but their provision is modelled as a residual rather than as deliberate decisions of individuals. Under the assumption of common mortality, when all individuals are assumed to die aged 80, this approach implies that there are no bequests. The final allocation of resources at the time of retirement is to consumption. All money remaining after the above provisions for income and investment is spent immediately.

Given the complexity of the system, there is in principle an infinitely large number of routes which may be taken at retirement. This chapter uses the 46 routes through the maze as described in chapter 11; route 47 is omitted from consideration in this chapter. The defined benefit is specified in relation to average earnings in the three years immediately before retirement; this average is referred to as the 'final salary'.

It is assumed that the age pension becomes payable only at age 65, and no provision is made for other social transfer payments. Thus, those retiring earlier than the age pension eligibility age must rely entirely on their own resources to provide income. They may be eligible to receive the low-income earners rebate, in addition to a rebate linked to the age pension.

Fringe benefits associated with the age pension or low income levels are not modelled. It would be difficult to make such allowance in a reasonable way, since such benefits reflect to a large extent the consumption pattern as well as the income level of an individual. However, the inclusion of such an allowance would exaggerate rather than moderate the incentives revealed below, since it would be inclined to increase the relative value of the low annuity income and high consumption options; options which are already preferred by the low-income and high-mortality groups.

12.1.2 Evaluation of Retirement Choice

The criterion for evaluating the retirement choice is specified in terms of a utility function based on net consumption and leisure in each year. Total leisure available in each year is normalised to unity, so that leisure is specified as a proportion of the available time. During retirement years this proportion is set equal to one in each year, and for working years it is set equal to a fixed value less than one (the sensitivity to this assumed value is examined below). If c_t and h_t respectively denote the amount of consumption and the proportion of time in leisure in year t, utility in that year is defined as the Cobb-Douglas form:

$$U_t = c_t^\alpha h_t^{1-\alpha} \tag{12.1}$$

where $\alpha < 1$. If there is a bequest, its value is added to consumption in the final year of life. Lifetime utility is then defined as the present value, at entry to the workforce, of the stream U_t.

Individuals are assumed not to save from any disposable income during retirement. The amount of net consumption in any year in retirement is the sum of income from any purchased annuities, plus the age pension received where relevant, plus the amount taken from the bank account, less the amount of income tax paid, allowing for the appropriate income tax rebates due. This amount is not the same, in general, as the net income in the year. Net income includes the interest earned on the bank account, but does not include the capital amount withdrawn from it. The amount of the bequest, if any, is the balance of the bank account at the time of death. Since the bank account is reduced to zero by age 80, any individual who survives this age provides no bequest.

It is necessary to stress that the evaluation of each route for each individual is made *ex post*. That is, the criterion refers to the consumption stream and bequest actually received by the individual over the whole of the retirement period. These results do not therefore directly indicate which routes are optimal *ex ante*, since it would be necessary to model explicitly the formation of expectations by individuals about the length of life.

12.1.3   Annuity Rates

Individuals who retire early and purchase an annuity receive benefits over a longer period than if they retire later. The purchase rate of annuities depends on the age from which they become payable. The current rate in Australia for a whole-life annuity escalating at 5 per cent per year for a male aged 65 is 12.5, so the cost of an annuity which pays $1 in the first year on retirement at age 65 is $12.50. Annuity purchase rates have been constructed for other ages consistent with this base value. This was done using the software package ADVANCE (Actuarial and Demographic, Visual And Numerical Curricula Enhancement) developed at the University of Melbourne.

The market for whole-life annuities in Australia is currently small, but as the Superannuation Guarantee Charge matures it is expected, if the government intention is realised, that this market will increase to include individuals previously absent from the annuity market. Hence the mortality characteristics of those purchasing retirement annuities are expected to change. The following simulations therefore use purchase rates based on differing mortality assumptions. Two sets of rates are used in this study, as shown in Table 12.1.

The first set of annuity rates for early retirement, A1, assumes that the underlying mortality experience is that of typical annuitants, and is based on the mortality table a(90) males. Current rates would be expected to reflect the effects of self-selection exercised by purchasers of annuities. On this mortality assumption, a purchase price of 12.5 at age 65 implies an underlying real rate of interest of 1.90 per cent allowing for escalation at 5

Table 12.1: Annuity Purchase Rates

Age	A1	A2
55	17.57	16.92
56	17.04	16.40
57	16.52	15.87
58	16.00	15.35
59	15.48	14.83
60	14.97	14.32
61	14.47	13.80
62	13.97	13.30
63	13.48	12.80
64	12.99	12.30
65	12.50	11.81

per cent. Assuming that all expense allowances and other costs are implicitly allowed for in this real rate of interest, ADVANCE was used to calculate the corresponding rates for ages 55-64, on the basis of the a(90) males mortality table.

The second set of annuity rates, A2, is based on the same real rate of interest implied by current market rates, that is 1.90 per cent, but uses a different assumption of mortality experience, the Australian Life Tables 1985-87, males. This mortality table is representative of a wider population than the annuitants mortality table used for the first set of rates, and the mortality rates are in general higher.

Annuitants' mortality is lower than the general population since it represents a group self-selecting on the basis of expectation of survival. If the purchase of retirement annuities becomes much more common than it is at present, then purchase rates would be expected to reflect the higher mortality experience of a wider group of purchasers of annuities. Thus, the second set of purchase rates is intended to be representative of market rates which might apply when the Superannuation Guarantee Charge scheme is mature and the purchase of retirement annuities is much more widespread than it is at present.

12.2   Simulation Results

The simulation model is used to simulate the lifetime experience of each of 3,000 individuals. In each case the value of discounted lifetime utility, based on the Cobb-Douglas form, is evaluated for each of the 46 routes through the maze and each retirement age from 55 to 65, and the combination of age and route giving the maximum value of utility is recorded. The simulation is carried out both for the assumption of common mortality, such that all individuals livè to age 80, and for differential mortality whereby the relatively richer live, on average, relatively longer (and the expectation of life for the median individual is 80 years). Any effect which early retirement may have on life expectancy is not modelled.

The choice of values of h_t (the proportion of time spent in leisure during each year) and α must be somewhat arbitrary. All that can be done is to choose sensible values as a base case and then to consider the sensitivity of results to variations. The coefficient α is the exponent on consumption. The form of U_t implies that, within each year, utility is constant if a 1 per cent increase in leisure is matched by a reduction in consumption of $\{(1 - \alpha)/\alpha\}$ per cent. Hence if α is set at 0.5, a 1 per cent increase in h_t accompanied by a 1 per cent reduction in c_t results in no change in utility. If α is increased to 0.6, for example, an increase in h_t of 1 per cent must be matched by a reduction in c_t of 0.667 per cent to maintain the same utility, reflecting a higher weight attached to consumption. If α is instead 0.4, a similar change in h_t implies a fall in consumption of 1.5 per cent if utility is to be constant. The central value of $\alpha = 0.5$ is taken as the base case, along with the assumption that $h_t = 0.25$ during each of the working years. After retirement a value of $h_t = 1$ is used.

12.2.1   Common Mortality

Tables 12.2 and 12.3 show respectively the optimal route choices for the A1 and A2 annuity rates, and the base values of $h_t = 0.25$ and $\alpha = 0.5$, on an assumption of common mortality (CM). Each table shows the number of members of the cohort selecting each age and route combination.

Table 12.2: Optimal Choices: Common Mortality (A1)

Route	55	56	57	58	59	60	61	62	63	64	65
1	11	-	-	-	-	-	-	-	-	-	-
2	25	-	-	-	-	-	-	-	-	-	-
5	69	51	10	2	-	3	1	-	-	-	-
8	24	6	1	1	-	-	-	-	-	-	-
9	17	28	28	33	40	23	17	-	-	-	-
12	166	207	197	105	19	20	20	22	23	8	4
15	26	32	57	79	143	225	207	113	27	2	-
16	2	3	6	13	44	106	129	135	85	25	1
19	10	10	6	1	-	-	-	-	-	-	-
22	-	-	-	-	1	3	21	38	24	15	2
25	63	35	17	7	14	15	12	10	4	3	4
28	15	13	3	-	-	-	-	-	-	-	-
35	13	-	-	-	-	-	-	-	-	-	-
Total	441	385	325	240	261	395	407	318	163	53	12

Table 12.3: Optimal Choices: Common Mortality (A2)

Route	55	56	57	58	59	60	61	62	63	64	65
1	12	-	-	-	-	-	-	-	-	-	-
2	35	-	-	-	-	-	-	-	-	-	-
5	90	55	39	7	7	11	3	3	-	1	1
8	24	10	5	6	-	-	-	-	-	-	-
9	19	25	35	34	56	43	27	13	1	-	-
12	171	210	214	119	38	11	15	17	14	3	3
15	19	15	45	60	116	199	224	105	35	6	-
16	5	4	2	5	25	49	79	93	72	15	-
19	5	6	8	-	-	-	-	-	-	-	-
22	-	-	-	-	-	-	4	12	12	7	2
25	107	52	33	23	25	22	36	22	12	14	6
28	11	9	5	-	-	-	-	-	-	-	-
35	17	-	-	-	-	-	-	-	-	-	-
Total	515	386	386	254	267	335	388	265	146	46	12

The essential features of the two tables are the same. The most preferred retirement age is 55, with a second mode at age 61. The preferred routes all involve using a proportion of the available funds to purchase an annuity and allow for the immediate consumption of any cash balance. Of the routes chosen, all (apart from 25, 28 and 35) are defined benefit routes and all involve the consumption of the balance of funds after the defined level of income has been met. These results, because based on common mortality experience, do not favour any use of the bank account, since the persisting capital value of this as an estate is only relevant when individuals die before age 80. The lower annuity purchase rates A2 involve more individuals taking routes 5, 9 and 25, and fewer taking routes 16 and 22, compared with the rates A1. Later comparisons are therefore shown only for the set A1.

The results shown in Tables 12.2 and 12.3 reflect the combined action of different effects and there is no single reason which explains the pattern of choices. A more detailed study was made of individuals and their optimal choice and, from the detail, it was found that patterns emerge. Looking at the defined benefit choices, it appears that the major part of the cohort are opting to buy a level of income which maximises their receipt of the means-tested age pension. Thus, in general, those choosing to retire with 50 per cent of final (average three years) salary rather than 35 per cent, for example, are retiring with similar levels of annuity income, but have a lower average salary over the final three years of work. Some routes purchase an annuity of the same proportion of final average salary (for example, the pairs of routes 5 and 8, 12 and 15, 19 and 22) but from different sources (using pre- or post-tax money). These pairs of routes differ only in the tax treatment of the annuity income purchased and the way in which the annuity is treated for the purposes of the age pension means-test. Routes 12 and 19 are preferred by those retiring earlier, whereas routes 15 and 22 are preferred by those who retire relatively later. Hence those retiring later find it advantageous to take their superannuation assets as a lump sum (and pay any tax if appropriate) before purchasing an annuity.

Consider the money purchase routes chosen. Route 28 allows for all superannuation benefits to be put to annuity purchase and the balance of assets to be spent immediately. This route is, effectively, preferred by individuals whose optimal percentage salary replacement is not represented in the defined benefit options. Similarly route 35 and route 25, which provide for all assets to be used to purchase annuity income, are distinguished by the fact that route 25 involves all superannuation assets being used to purchase an annuity, and route 35 specifies taking a lump sum and using after-tax money to purchase an annuity. Thus, the optimal routes chosen fall into associated pairs, and each member of the pair is distinguished by the associated tax and means-test operation.

The general trend is that those whose income level is such that the operation of the age pension means-test may have an effect, purchase a level of income which will maximise their benefit. This constitutes the majority of the cohort: this majority arranges affairs such that they just get under the means-test thresholds.

There is a small group whose level of earnings are so low that the workings of the means-tests are irrelevant, because they are never able to purchase an income in excess of the thresholds. For this group, the optimal behaviour is to retire as early as possible, since there is no relative advantage in remaining in low-paid employment.

There is another small class of individuals who are always able to purchase income well in excess of the means-test thresholds. These individuals arrange their net income according to the relationship between the annuity purchase rates and their level of income.

The effects on the optimal retirement age of changing the values of α and h_t from the base case are straightforward. The effect of increasing α alone, that is, attaching more weight to consumption compared with leisure, is to reduce the extent of early retirement. However, a less obvious result is that the importance of different routes through the maze changes substantially. With $\alpha = 0.6$, very few select routes 12, 5, and 27. Those retiring in their early sixties select mainly routes 8 and 9, along with 35. Later retirees prefer 25 and 44. The higher value of α also eliminates the bimodality in the distribution of optimal age at retirement. Increasing h_t to 0.3 does not eliminate the bimodality. The effect of a higher value of h_t during the working

Table 12.4: Universal Pension: Common Mortality (A1)

Route	55	56	57	58	59	60	61	62	63	64	65
1	13	1	-	-	-	-	-	-	-	-	-
2	36	6	3	-	-	-	-	-	-	-	-
5	83	99	120	117	79	35	7	-	-	-	-
9	-	1	-	5	3	1	1	-	-	-	-
12	94	159	266	324	364	294	170	121	64	13	2
15	-	-	-	-	-	-	-	1	1	2	1
16	-	-	-	1	-	-	1	-	-	15	3
19	1	-	1	3	2	8	3	1	1	-	1
22	-	-	-	-	-	-	-	-	-	1	2
25	36	26	47	46	64	41	27	29	4	4	3
28	1	-	4	13	24	38	34	12	10	4	-
35	-	-	-	-	-	-	-	-	-	-	2
Total	265	292	441	509	536	417	243	164	80	39	14

life is to produce a movement towards later retirement ages, resulting from the smaller increase in leisure on retirement, but there is little effect on the optimal choice of route.

12.2.2   A Universal Pension

The above results suggest that a substantial proportion of individuals in the cohort are affected by the age pension means-test, which influences not only the allocation of assets but also the age of retirement. It is therefore useful to examine the effects of abolishing the means-test. Table 12.4 shows that the optimal choice of the same cohort under conditions which are the same as those for Table 12.2, except that the age pension is universal and subject to no means-testing. The differences in choice are thus entirely due to the removal of the means-test. Obviously, those few individuals beneath the effects of the means-test do not change their behaviour. The distribution of retirement ages becomes unimodal with the universal age pension. This eliminates the mode at the lowest age, but the single mode is slightly lower than the highest mode when there is means-testing. The arithmetic mean optimal retirement age is the same in each case, at 59 years.

The result is that the removal of means-testing leads more individuals to replace a higher proportion of income and/or to retire later. The majority of the cohort is within the reach of the existing age-pension means-test and, when this is removed, these people are encouraged to purchase higher levels of income and to work longer in order to do so.

Comparison of Tables 12.2 and 12.4 also shows that almost all of those choosing to buy annuities with after-tax money rather than directly from superannuation, in Table 12.2, were doing so because the means-test distinguishes between them rather than because the income tax rules make a distinction. With a universal pension, very few continue to choose routes 8, 15, 19 and 22. Similarly, more choose routes 25 and 28.

One argument made against the introduction of a universal pension is that it involves higher expenditure. However, the results presented here show that, in the context of early retirement choices, the universal pension produces an incentive for higher levels of income provision and an associated delay in retirement age. This incentive may give rise to additional taxation to offset the costs of a universal pension.

12.2.3 Differential Mortality

Tables 12.5 and 12.6 show the optimal choices of the members of the cohort when subject to differential rather than common mortality, for annuity routes A1. Thus differences between the pair of Tables 12.2 and 12.4, and the pair 12.3 and 12.6 arise entirely from the change in mortality assumption. As might be expected, routes involving the bank account are chosen under the assumption of differential mortality. Those who die before the age of 80 retain a capital asset by using the bank account and would otherwise, if purchasing an annuity, experience a loss due to mortality.

With differential mortality there is also a drift towards retirement at the later ages (particularly 64 and 65), though the broad bimodal pattern is still observed, with modes again at age 55 and 61. The general pattern is unchanged, but those with mortality much higher than the average choose the bank options, and those whose longevity significantly exceeds the norm choose higher levels of annuity purchase. The number of individuals choosing Route 25 (all assets used to purchase an annuity) doubles.

Another major difference when there is differential mortality is that some of the money purchase routes, notably 27, 35, 43 and 44, become optimal for a significant minority of the cohort. Further analysis of individuals and their characteristics suggest the following patterns. First, the money purchase routes involving bank accounts are only used by those of below-average life expectancy, who leave an estate. Secondly, route 25, the 100 per cent annuity route, is strongly favoured by high-income, high-longevity individuals. Thirdly, earlier retirement ages are typically associated with those on low earnings, and with low ages of survival.

A general result with differential mortality is that the lower the earnings, the earlier the preferred age at retirement and vice versa. Thus the introduction of differential mortality has the following general effects by comparison with common mortality. First, individuals with high incomes and low mortality are inclined to buy more annuity income and retire later. Secondly, individuals with low incomes and high mortality are inclined to buy less annuity income and retire earlier. The net effect is a flattening of the distribution of the age of retirement. This is a complimentary net effect to that of introducing a universal pension.

The two fringe classes who lie outside the means-test influence are simply able to buy a higher level of income than before. The lower purchase rates result in a slight shift in that some will be brought up into the range of income influenced by the means-test and some will rise beyond it. Table 12.7 shows results of combining a universal pension with differential mortality. Again, the universal pension eliminates the lowest mode.

12.2.4 Earnings Profiles

It was suggested above that a factor in the determination of the optimum retirement age, in addition to the tax and transfer structure, is the shape of the individual's earnings profile. The benefits of an extra year's earnings must be balanced against those of an extra year of leisure in retirement and

Table 12.5: Optimal Choices: Differential Mortality (A1)

Route	55	56	57	58	59	60	61	62	63	64	65
1	7	-	-	-	-	-	-	-	-	-	-
2	19	1	-	-	-	-	-	-	1	-	-
3	-	-	-	-	-	-	-	-	-	-	-
4	4	-	-	-	-	-	-	-	-	-	-
5	49	34	13	10	1	4	2	1	2	-	1
7	4	-	-	-	-	-	-	-	-	-	-
8	13	1	1	1	3	7	22	28	10	1	1
9	15	13	8	4	13	27	53	56	19	3	2
11	34	-	-	-	-	-	-	-	-	-	-
12	124	144	128	45	6	3	3	2	1	-	2
14	4	1	-	-	-	-	-		-	-	-
15	17	29	32	26	44	75	85	72	37	13	4
16	6	8	13	21	41	55	70	61	36	19	5
18	47	52	56	49	10	-	2	3	-	-	-
19	7	10	4	3	-	-	-	-	-	-	-
21	-	-	1	-	3	4	6	1		3	-
22	-	-	-	2	2	7	12	22	5	5	-
25	35	31	29	5	5	14	21	33	44	30	110
27	22	14	3	3	-	-	-	-	-	-	-
28	7	7	2	-	-	-	-	1	-	-	-
30	8	3	19	39	36	25	1	1	-	-	-
33	-	-	2	2	1	-	-	-	-	-	-
35	1	-	-	-	-	-	3	8	1	-	3
38	10	1	2	-	2	5	5	5	1	-	1
40	-	-	-	-	-	-	1	8	15	4	-
43	-	-	6	17	39	63	68	32	8	5	-
44	-	-	-	-	-	-	-	-		31	66
Total	433	349	319	227	206	289	354	334	214	146	129

Table 12.6: Optimal Choices: Differential Mortality (A2)

Route	55	56	57	58	59	60	61	62	63	64	65
1	7	-	-	-	-	-	-	-	-	-	-
2	30	-	3	-	1	-	1	1	1	1	-
5	68	37	35	12	3	2	4	4	3	-	1
7	3	-	-	-	-	-	-	-	-	-	-
8	21	2	3	1	4	9	31	35	6	2	-
9	15	11	8	8	12	17	41	57	33	9	3
11	41	1	-	-	-	-	-	-	-	-	-
12	149	145	140	74	15	2	3	2	2	-	2
14	5	-	-	1	-	-	-	-	-	-	-
15	27	14	25	26	45	54	87	46	29	8	4
16	6	10	11	13	29	41	53	40	31	7	2
18	57	35	49	43	17	2	2	2	-	-	-
19	7	6	9	1	-	-	-	-	-	-	-
21	-	2	-	-	1	1	1	3	-	-	-
22	-	-	-	2	2	1	6	12	6	1	1
25	62	34	47	23	11	17	32	35	53	41	131
27	32	12	11	5	-	-	-	-	-	-	-
28	8	5	5	3	-	-	1	1	-	-	-
30	-	7	12	21	27	22	3	-	-	-	-
33	-	-	2	1	1	-	-	-	-	-	-
35	2	-	-	-	-	1	1	7	5	1	1
38	16	-	1	2	-	3	4	4	-	-	-
40	-	-	-	-	-	-	-	9	8	2	-
43	-	-	1	4	28	54	54	20	1	3	-
44	-	-	-	-	-	-	-	-	31	64	-
Total	560	321	362	240	196	226	324	278	209	139	145

Table 12.7: Universal Pension: Differential Mortality (A1)

Route	55	56	57	58	59	60	61	62	63	64	65
1	6	-	-	-	-	-	-	-	-	-	-
2	23	2	9	9	6	4	3	2	1	-	-
4	4	-	-	-	-	-	-	-	-	-	-
5	64	46	47	58	39	32	16	21	7	5	-
9	2	2	-	1	1	-	-	-	-	-	-
11	28	2	-	1	-	-	-	-	-	-	-
12	101	123	183	151	143	119	70	39	17	6	2
14	1	-	-	-	-	-	-	-	-	-	-
16	-	-	1	1	-	-	-	-	-	1	-
18	39	33	46	46	34	30	15	5	2	2	1
19	2	2	3	7	5	10	4	2	-	-	-
25	16	21	31	56	73	102	86	84	61	47	98
27	41	25	18	12	7	4	-	-	-	-	-
28	9	5	23	23	34	32	21	11	1	1	-
30	3	2	2	1	3	12	9	14	6	4	-
33	-	-	-	3	8	6	8	1	1	1	-
38	6	-	-	-	-	-	-	-	-	-	-
43	-	-	6	14	39	57	55	24	3	8	-
44	-	-	-	-	-	-	-	1	25	49	-
Total	345	263	369	383	392	408	287	204	124	124	101

Table 12.8: Steeper Earnings Profiles: Common Mortality (A1)

Route	55	56	57	58	59	60	61	62	63	64	65
2	2	-	-	-	-	-	-	-	-	-	-
5	9	12	3	-	1	1	2	-	-	-	-
8	1	2	1	-	1	-	-	-	-	-	-
9	3	7	6	10	9	17	7	2	-	-	-
12	45	53	69	68	10	17	29	46	51	52	57
15	-	6	15	30	68	149	211	143	55	20	-
16	-	2	3	6	17	58	165	269	203	115	14
19	-	4	1	-	-	-	-	-	-	-	10
22	-	-	-	-	-	5	44	116	163	193	75
25	13	5	8	2	9	15	21	18	18	11	95
28	2	5	5	-	-	-	-	-	-	-	-
35	2	-	-	-	-	-	-	-	-	-	8
38	-	-	-	-	-	-	-	-	-	1	9
Total	77	96	111	116	115	262	479	594	490	392	268

the impact of the means-tested pension. Each individual in the simulations experiences a unique earnings profile, based on the use of a stochastic model of earnings estimated using Australian data and described in chapter 10. The model implies that, on average, those with relatively higher earnings experience their peak earnings relatively later than those with relatively lower earnings; for further discussion of this phenomenon, see Creedy (1985, p.68). The parameters used in the above simulations imply, however, that an individual who experiences the median income of the cohort in each year of working life receives peak real earnings at about age 50 years, although nominal median earnings never fall over the relevant period. Arithmetic mean real earnings reach a peak about 3.5 years later.

It is therefore worth considering the effects of somewhat steeper age-earnings profiles. Simulations were accordingly carried out for alternative parameters; the values of θ and δ were changed to 0.04 and 0.0006. These imply that the median value of real earnings reaches a peak at about 62 years. The upper deciles reach a maximum substantially later, of course. Results are given in Table 12.8 for common mortality and annuity purchase rates A1. As expected, the modal age of retirement increases and the lower mode disappears, although there remains a substantial amount of early retirement.

The effect of making the age pension universal is that the distribution of age at retirement becomes more widely dispersed. The mode falls by one year although the lower tail contains fewer people. The average optimal retirement age is 61 for both means-tested and universal systems, however. Routes 25 and 28 become substantially more popular, especially among late retirees, as does route 12. The number for whom routes 15 and 16 are optimal falls dramatically; these involve the taking of lump sums (before purchasing an annuity) and consuming all that remains after purchasing a specified proportion (50 and 45 per cent respectively) of final salary, and are obviously driven by the existence of the means-tests.

12.2.5 Contribution Rates

An important issue, not mentioned so far, concerns the desirable level of the contribution rates in a mandated superannuation scheme such as the Superannuation Guarantee Charge. The scheme is introduced on the (paternalistic) argument that individuals are generally myopic and will not otherwise save enough for retirement. However, there is a possibility that some people are thereby forced to 'oversave'; decreasing marginal utility implies a preference for a smooth consumption stream. Contribution rates that are 'too high' tend to encourage early retirement rather than higher consumption during retirement. Any attempt to increase aggregate savings with such a mandatory scheme would thus be frustrated. It is therefore of interest to examine the implications of a mature scheme in which individuals are faced with lower contribution rates and save less out of disposable income in each year of the working life.

Suppose that the employee and employer contribution rates are reduced to 2 and 6 per cent respectively (from the 3 and 9 per cent used above), and that individuals reduce their additional saving rate to 2.5 per cent (from 5 per cent assumed above). With the base values of $h_t = 0.25$ and $\alpha = 0.5$, and using the annuity rates A1, the average optimal age at retirement, with common mortality, is increased to 62, with the (single) mode increasing to age 64 (when almost a third of the cohort retire). The choice of routes through the maze is dominated by routes 15, 16 and 22 (the most popular among the late retirers). Each of these defined benefit routes involves the superannuation assets being taken as a lump sum before an annuity is purchased (to achieve 50, 45 and 35 per cent respectively of the average earnings over the final three working years), with the remaining assets (if any) being consumed at retirement.

The fact that the bank account is not used is driven by the assumptions of common mortality and the draw-down of the account, but it is likely that the use of the lump sums is driven by the tax treatment of annuities and the means-test for the age pension. Where the age pension is universal, the average optimal retirement age is reduced by one year to 61, which in this case is also the mode. With a universal pension the optimal routes are dominated instead by 12, 19 and 28 since individuals are not penalised for replacing a higher level of income. The two defined benefit routes 12 and 19 use pre-tax money to purchase an annuity, while route 28 involves all superanuation funds being used to purchase an annuity and all additional savings being consumed at retirement.

The alternative assumption of differential mortality introduces, as before, a richer range of optimal routes through the maze as more of the money purchase alternatives become optimal and the use of a bank account in retirement is more common. With differential mortality the average age at retirement continues to be 62 (with the mode at 64). Routes 15, 16 and 22 continue to be popular (as with common mortality), though the money purchase routes 40, 43 and 44, which involve the use of a bank account and possible bequests, are frequently used (the modal combination of age and route is in fact age 64 and route 44). The latter two routes do not involve the purchase of an annuity. The choice of routes 15 and 16 is clearly driven by the means-test relating to the age pension; with a universal pension these routes virtually disappear and routes 25 and 28 become very popular, with 30 and 33 also being used more frequently. In this case the universal pension has the same mean and modal optimal retirement age, but the distribution is, as usual, more widely dispersed. The question of the appropriate contribution rate (along with the profile of the rate over the life cycle) warrants further investigation.

12.3 Conclusions

This chapter used a lifetime simulation model in order to examine the optimal choice both of the retirement age (between the ages of 55 and 65) and the allocation of assets at retirement, involving the route through what has been referred to as the retirement maze. Each simulated member of the cohort was assumed to maximise a lifetime utility function defined in terms of the present value of utility, with each year's utility independently defined as a Cobb-Douglas function of consumption and leisure in the year.

In view of the fact that individuals' preferences are not known and the simulation model requires a number of strong simplifications and assumptions, the results must be treated with caution. However, they suggest the existence of a significant incentive towards early retirement and a substantial impact of the age pension means-tests on the allocation of resources and optimal retirement age of individuals. The extent and nature of incentives were found to vary with the mortality assumption used, and depend on the means-tests associated with the age pension. The assumptions of a universal pension encourages later retirement in a substantial proportion of the cohort. The simulations apply to a fully mature Superannuation Guarantee Charge scheme, such that the contribution rates apply for each year of the working life. This will not apply until individuals are retiring after approximately the year 2040.

The analysis also raised the question of the appropriate level of contribution rates in a mandated scheme. Results suggest that lower contribution rates encourage a later preferred retirement age.

Bibliography

[1] Aaron, H. (1966) The social insurance paradox. *Canadian Journal of Economics*, 2, pp. 371-379.

[2] Aitchison, J.A. and Brown, J.A.C. (1957) *The Lognormal Distribution.* Cambridge: Cambridge University Press.

[3] Alvarado, J. and Creedy, J. (1995) Migration and population ageing in Australia. *Australian Bulletin of Labour*, 21, pp. 32-47.

[4] Alvarado, J. and Creedy, J. (1997) *Population Ageing, Migration and Social Expenditure.* Aldershot: Edward Elgar.

[5] Atkinson, A.B. (1970) On the measurement of inequality. *Journal of Economic Theory*, 1, pp. 244-263.

[6] Atkinson, A.B. (1987) Income maintenance and social insurance. In *Handbook of Public Economics*, Vol. II (ed. by A.J. Auerbach and M. Feldstein), pp. 779-908. New York: North-Holland.

[7] Atkinson, A.B. and Stiglitz, J.E. (1980) *Lectures in Public Economics.* New York: McGraw Hill.

[8] Atkinson, M.E. and Creedy, J. (1996) Modelling optimal retirement decisions in Australia. *Australian Economic Papers*, 35, pp. 39-59.

[9] Atkinson, M.E. and Creedy, J. (1997) The choice of early retirement age and the Australian superannuation system. *Australian Journal of Labour Economics,* 1, pp. 1-23.

[10] Atkinson, M.E., Creedy, J. and Knox, D.M. (1995) An equity analysis of some radical suggestions for Australia's retirement income system. *Quarterly Journal of The Institute of Actuaries of Australia*, June, pp. 2-25.

[11] Atkinson, M.E., Creedy, J. and Knox, D.M. (1995) Planning retirement income in Australia: routes through the maze. *Australian Economic Review*, 4, pp. 15-28.

[12] Atkinson, M.E., Creedy, J. and Knox, D.M. (1996) Alternative retirement income strategies: a cohort analysis of lifetime redistribution. *Economic Record*, 72, pp. 97-106.

[13] Australian Bureau of Statistics (1988) *The Labour Force Australia, June.* Catalogue no. 6203. Canberra: ABS.

[14] Australian Bureau of Statistics (1989-90) *Australian National Accounts, Gross Product, Employment and Hours Worked.* Catalogue no. 5211. Canberra: ABS.

[15] Australian Bureau of Statistics (1989a) *Projections of the Populations of Australia States and Territories 1989 to 2031.* Catalogue no. 3222.0. Canberra: ABS.

[16] Australian Bureau of Statistics (1989b) *Projections of the Population of Australia States and Territories 1989 to 2031.* Catalogue no. 3222.0. Canberra: ABS.

[17] Australian Bureau of Statistics (1989c) *Estimated Resident Population by Sex and Age: States and Territories of Australia, June 1988 and Preliminary June 1989.* Catalogue no. 3201. Canberra: ABS.

[18] Australian Bureau of Statistics (1989d) *Overseas Born Australians 1988: a Statistical Profile.* Catalogue no. 4112.0 ABS Canberra: ABS.

[19] Australian Bureau of Statistics (1990) *Estimated Resident Population by Country of Birth, Age and Sex, Australia.* Catalogue no. 3221.0. Canberra: ABS.

[20] Australian Bureau of Statistics (1991a) *Births Australia.* Catalogue no. 3301.0. Canberra: ABS.

[21] Australian Bureau of Statistics (1992) *Labour Force Survey* (unpublished data). Canberra: ABS.

[22] Barber, J., Moon, G. and Doolan, S. (1994) *Targeting for Equity.* Canberra: Ageing Agendas, AGPS.

[23] Bateman, H. and Piggott, J. (1992) Australian retirement income policy. *Australian Tax Forum,* 9, pp. 1-26.

[24] Bateman, H., Frisch, J., Kingston, G. and Piggott, J. (1991) Demographics, retirement saving and superannuation policy: an Australian perspective. In *Saving and Policy* (ed. by P.J. Stemp), pp. 193-227. Canberra: CEPR.

[25] Bateman, H., Kingston, G. and Piggott, J. (1993) Taxes, retirement transfers and annuities. *Economic Record,* 69, pp. 274-284.

[26] Bateman, H., Kingston, G. and Piggott, J. (1994) The equity implications of mandated funded pension schemes. In *Taxation, Poverty and Income Distribution* (ed. by J. Creedy), pp. 163-174. Aldershot: Edward Elgar.

[27] Bell, M. (1992) *Demographic Projections and Forecasts in Australia: a Directory and Digest.* Canberra: AGPS.

[28] Blake, D. (1992) *Issues in Pension Funding.* London: Routledge.

[29] Breit, W. (1974). Income redistribution and efficiency norms. In *Redistribution Through Public Choice* (ed. by H.M. Hochman and G.E. Peterson), pp. 3-21. New York: Columbia University Press.

[30] Brown, C. (1980) Equalising differences in the labour market. *Quarterly Journal of Economics,* pp. 113-134.

[31] Bureau of Immigration and Population Research (1991) *Community Profiles*. Canberra: AGPS.

[32] Bureau of Immigration and Population Research (1992) *Australia's Population Trends and Prospects*. Canberra: AGPS.

[33] Cameron, L. and Creedy, J. (1995) Indirect tax exemptions and the distribution of lifetime income: a simulation analysis. *Economic Record*, 71, pp. 77-87.

[34] Carney, T. and Hanks, P. (1994) *Social Security in Australia*. Melbourne: Oxford University Press.

[35] Cipolla, C.M. (1965) *The Economic History of World Population*. Harmondsworth: Penguin Books.

[36] Clark, R.L. and Spengler, J.J. (1980) *The Economics of Individual and Population Ageing*. Cambridge: Cambridge University Press.

[37] Commonwealth Department of Community Services and Health, Policy Development Division (1990) *The Impact of Population Ageing on Commonwealth and State Social Outlays 1987-1988*. Canberra: AGPS.

[38] Cox, P.R. (1971) *Demography*. Cambridge: Cambridge University Press.

[39] Creedy, J. (1982). *State Pensions in Britain*. Cambridge: Cambridge University Press.

[40] Creedy, J. (1985) *Dynamics of Income Distribution*. Oxford: Basil Blackwell.

[41] Creedy, J. (1991) Lifetime earnings of men in Australia. *Journal of Industrial Relations*, pp. 41-52.

[42] Creedy, J. (1992) *Income, Inequality and the Life Cycle*. Aldershot: Edward Elgar.

[43] Creedy, J. (1994a) Pensions and compensating wage variations. *Scottish Journal of Political Economy*, 41, pp. 454-463.

[44] Creedy, J. (1994b) Two-tier state pensions: labour supply and income distribution. *The Manchester School*, LXII, pp. 167-183.

[45] Creedy, J. (1995) (ed.) *The Economics of Ageing*. Aldershot: Edward Elgar.

[46] Creedy, J. (1996) *Fiscal Policy and Social Welfare: An Analysis of Alternative Tax and Transfer Schemes*. Aldershot: Edward Elgar.

[47] Creedy, J. (1997) Measuring inequality and tax progressivity with alternative income concepts. *Review of Income and Wealth*, 43, pp. 283-295.

[48] Creedy, J. and Disney, R. (1985) *Social Insurance in Transition*. Oxford: Basil Blackwell.

[49] Creedy, J. and Disney, R. (1989a) Can we afford to grow older? Population ageing and social security. *European Economic Review*, 33, pp. 367-376.

[50] Creedy, J. and Disney, R. (1989b) The Australian pension scheme: some basic analytics. *Economic Record*, 65, pp. 357-368.

[51] Creedy, J. and Disney, R. (1989c) The new pension scheme in Britain. In *The Economics of Social Security*. (ed. by A. Dilnot and I. Walker), pp. 224-239. Oxford: Oxford University Press.

[52] Creedy, J. and Disney, R. (1990) Pension schemes and incentives: case studies from Australia and the UK. *Australian Economic Review*, 1, pp. 23-31.

[53] Creedy, J. and Disney, R. (1992) Financing pensions in alternative pay-as-you-go pension schemes. *Bulletin of Economic Research*, 44, pp. 39-53.

[54] Creedy, J., Disney, R. and Whitehouse, E. (1992) The earnings-related state pension: indexation and lifetime redistribution in the UK. *Review of Income and Wealth*, 39, pp. 257-278.

[55] Creedy, J. and Morgan, M. (1993) Pension and tax structures in an ageing population. *Journal of Economic Studies*, 19, pp. 50-65.

[56] Creedy, J. and Morgan, M. (1995) Policy trade-offs in alternative tax and pension systems. *Australian Economic Papers*, 34, pp. 332-344.

[57] Creedy, J. and Taylor, P. (1993) Population ageing and social expenditure in Australia. *Australian Economic Review*, 3, pp. 44-56.

[58] Creedy, J. and van de Ven, J. (1997) Retirement incomes: private savings versus social transfers. *University of Melbourne Department of Economics Research Paper*, no. 569.

[59] Dawkins, J. (1992) *Security in Retirement*. Canberra: AGPS.

[60] Department of Employment Education and Training, Economic and Policy Analysis Division (1991) *Australia's Workforce in the Year 2001*. Canberra: AGPS.

[61] Diamond, P.A. (1977) A framework for social security analysis. *Journal of Public Economics*, 3, pp. 275-298.

[62] Dilnot, A. and Johnson, P. (1993) *The Taxation of Private Pensions*. London: Institute for Fiscal Studies.

[63] Dilnot, A., Disney, R., Johnson, P. and Whitehouse, E. (1994) *Pensions Policy in the UK*. London: Institute for Fiscal Studies.

[64] Disney, R. (1996) *Can We Afford to Grow Older?* Cambridge, Mass: The MIT Press.

[65] Economic Planning Advisory Council (1988) Economic Effects of an Ageing Population. *Council Paper no. 29.*

[66] Economic Planning Advisory Council (1994) Australia's Ageing Society. *Background Paper no. 37.*

[67] Ehrenberg, R.G. (1980) Retirement system characteristics and compensating wage differentials in the public sector. *Industrial and Labour Relations Review*, 33, pp. 470-484.

[68] FitzGerald, V. (1993) *National Saving.* Canberra: AGPS.

[69] Foster, C. (1988) *Towards a National Retirement Incomes Policy.* Canberra: Department of Social Security.

[70] Gilbert, B.B. (1966) *The Evolution of National Insurance in Great Britain.* London: Michael Joseph.

[71] Glass, D.V. (1973) (ed.) *The Population Controversy.* Aldershot: Gregg International Publishers.

[72] Gruen, F.H. (1985) Australian government policy on retirement incomes. *Economic Record*, 61, pp. 613-621.

[73] Gunderson, M., Hyatt, D. and Pesando, J.E. (1992) Wage-pension trade-offs in collective agreements. *Industrial and Labor Relations Review*, 46, pp. 146-60.

[74] Hagemann, R.P. and G. Nicoletti (1989) Ageing populations: economic effects and implications for public finance. *OECD, Department of Economics and Statistics Working Papers* no. 61.

[75] Hammermesh, D.S. (1985) Expectations, life expectancy and economic behaviour. *Quarterly Journal of Economics*, 100, pp. 398-408.

[76] Heller, P.S., Hemming, R. and Kohnert, P.W. (1986) *Ageing and Social Expenditure in the Major Industrial Countries 1980-2025.* Washington, DC: International Monetary Fund.

[77] Hogben, L. (1938) (ed.) *Political Arithmetic: A Symposium of Population Studies.* London: George Allen and Unwin.

[78] Hugo, G. (1992) Australia's contemporary and future fertility and mortality: trends differentials and implications. In *National Population Council: Population Issues and Australia's Future, Environment, Economy and Society*. Canberra: AGPS.

[79] Hwong, H., Reed, W.R. and Hubbard, C. (1992) Compensating wage differentials and unobserved productivity. *Journal of Political Economy*, 100, pp. 835-847.

[80] Institute of Actuaries of Australia (1994) *Submission to the Select Committee on Superannuation*. Sydney: Institute of Actuaries of Australia.

[81] James, P. (1979) *Population Malthus: His Life and Times*. London: Routledge and Kegan Paul.

[82] Jenkins, S. (1988) Calculating income distribution indices from microdata. *National Tax Journal*, XLI, pp. 139-142.

[83] Kakwani, N. (1980) *Inequality and poverty: Methods of Estimation and Policy Analysis*. Oxford: Oxford University Press.

[84] Kee, P. (1992) *Social and Economic Attainment of Immigrants and Later Generation Australians*. Canberra: AGPS.

[85] Kelley, A.C. (1988) Australia: the coming of age. *Australian Economic Review*, 2, pp. 27-44.

[86] Kennedy, B.R. (1990) Financial consistency in longitudinal microsimulation: homemaker pensions re-examined. *Review of Income and Wealth*, 2, pp. 215-222.

[87] Knox, D.M. (1990) *A Review of the Options for Taxing Superannuation*. Sydney: Australian Tax Research Foundation.

[88] Knox, D.M. (1995) The age pension: means tested or universal? *Australian Economic Review*, 3, pp. 107-110.

[89] Lambert, P.J. (1985) Endogenizing the income distribution: the redistributive effect and Laffer effects of a progressive tax-benefit system. *European Journal of Political Economy*, 1, pp. 3-20.

[90] Lambert, P.J. (1988) Okun's bucket: a leak and two splashes. *Journal of Economic Studies*, 1, pp. 71-78.

[91] Lambert, P.J. (1990) The equity-efficiency trade-off: Breit reconsidered. *Oxford Economic Papers*, 3, pp. 91-104.

[92] Lambert, P.J. (1993a) Evaluating impact effects of tax reforms. *Journal of Economic Surveys*, 7, pp. 205-242.

[93] Lambert, P.J. (1993b) *The Distribution and Redistribution of Income*. Manchester: Manchester University Press.

[94] Lazear, E.P. (1979) Why is there mandatory retirement? *Journal of Political Economy*, 87, pp. 1261-84.

[95] Malthus, T.R. (1926) *First Essay on Population* (with notes by J. Bonar). London: Macmillan.

[96] Masson, P.R. and R.W. Tryon (1990) Macroeconomic effects of projected population ageing in industrial countries. *IMF Staff Papers*, 37, pp. 453-485.

[97] McCleary, G.F. (1937) *The Menace of British Depopulation*. London: George Allen and Unwin.

[98] Mitchell, D., Harding, A. and Gruen, F. (1994) Targeting welfare: a survey. *Economic Record*, 70, pp. 315-340.

[99] National Population Council (1991) *Population Issues and Australia's Future*. Canberra: AGPS.

[100] National Population Council (1992) *Population Issues and Australia's Future, Environment, Economy and Society*. Canberra: AGPS.

[101] New South Wales Budget Papers (1987-8) *Budget Information: Budget Paper no. 2.*

[102] Northern Territory Budget Papers (1988-9) *Budget Detailed Estimates: Budget Paper no .4.*

[103] OECD (1988) *Ageing Populations: The Social Policy Implications.* Paris: OECD.

[104] Office of the Australian Government Actuary (1991) *Australian Life Tables 1985-1987.* Canberra: AGPS.

[105] Prest, A.R. (1970) Some redistributional aspects of the national superannuation scheme. *Three Banks Review*, 86, pp. 3-22.

[106] Queensland Budget Papers (1988-9) *Departmental Services and Programs: A Budget Perspective.* Queensland State Public Service, pp. 130-131.

[107] Reddaway, W.B. (1939) *The Economics of a Declining Population.* London: George Allen and Unwin.

[108] Revelle, R. (1971) (ed.) *Rapid Population Growth: Consequences and Policy Implications.* Baltimore: Johns Hopkins University Press.

[109] Rosen, S. (1984) Some arithmetic of social security. In *Controlling the Cost of Social Security* (ed. by C.D. Campbell), pp. 233-255. Lexington, Ma: Lexington Books.

[110] Rosen, S. (1986) The theory of equalising differences. In *Handbook of Labor Economics* (ed. by O. Ashenfelter and R. Layard), pp. 641-691. Amsterdam: North-Holland.

[111] Samuelson, P.A. (1958) An exact consumption-loan model of interest with or without the social contrivance of money. *Journal of Political Economy*, 66, pp. 467-482.

[112] Saunders, P. (1995) Improving work incentives in a means-tested welfare system: the 1994 Australian Social Security reforms. *Fiscal Studies*, 16, pp. 45-70.

[113] Sauvy, A. (1963) *Théories Générale de la Population* Vol. I. Paris: Presses Universitaires de France.

[114] Schiller, B.R. and Weiss, R.D. (1980) Pensions and wages: a test for equalizing differences. *Review of Economics and Statistics*, 62, pp. 529-538.

[115] Sen, A.K. (1973) *On Economic Inequality*. Oxford: Clarendon Press.

[116] Smith, R.S. (1981) Compensating differentials for pensions and underfunding in the public sector. *Review of Economics and Statistics*, 63, pp. 463-467.

[117] Smith, R.S. and Ehrenberg, R.G. (1983) Estimating wage-fringe trade-offs: some data problems. In *The Measurement of Labor Cost* (ed. by J.E. Triplett), pp. 347-367. Chicago: University of Chicago Press.

[118] Smith, R.W. (1979) Compensating wage differentials and public policy: a review. *Industrial and Labour Relations Review*, 32, pp. 339-352.

[119] South Australian Budget Papers (1988-9) *Estimates of Payments: Financial Paper no. 3*.

[120] Stone, R. (1971) *Demographic Accounting and Model-building*. Paris: OECD.

[121] Tasmania Budget Papers (1988-9) *Consolidated Fund Summary of Estimated Expenditure and Estimated Receipts: Budget Paper no. 2*.

[122] Victoria Budget Papers (1988-9) *Budget Summary and Program Budget Expenditures: Budget Paper no. 5*.

[123] Western Australian Budget Papers (1988-9) *Consolidated Revenue Fund: Estimates of Revenue and Expenditure for Year Ending June 1989*.

[124] Wooden, M. (1990) *Migrant Labour Market Status*. Canberra: AGPS.

[125] World Bank (1994) *Averting the Old Age Crisis*. New York: Oxford University Press.

[126] Yitzhaki, S. (1983) On an extension of the Gini index. *International Economic Review*, 24, pp. 617-621.

[127] Young, C. (1990) *Australia's Ageing Population: Policy Options*. Canberra: Bureau of Immigration Research, AGPS.

Index